THE SIKHS

LECTURES ON THE HISTORY OF RELIGION
Sponsored by the American Council of Learned Societies New Series
Number 14

THE
SIKHS

HISTORY, RELIGION, AND SOCIETY

W. H. McLeod

COLUMBIA UNIVERSITY PRESS

New York

COLUMBIA UNIVERSITY PRESS
NEW YORK   CHICHESTER, WEST SUSSEX

LIBRARY OF CONGRESS CATALOGING-IN-PUBLICATION DATA

McLeod, W. H.
The Sikhs : history, religion, and society.
(Lectures on the history of religions ; new ser., no. 14)
Bibliography: p.
Includes index.
1. Sikhs—History. 2. Sikhism. I. Title. II. Series.
DS485.P3M39   1989   909'.0882946   88-25620
ISBN 0-231-06815-8

Book Design by Jaya Dayal

Casebound editions of Columbia University Press books are
printed on permanent and durable acid-free paper

Printed in the United States of America

c 10 9 8 7 6 5 4 3 2 1
p 10 9 8 7 6 5 4 3 2

THIS volume is the fourteenth to be published in the series of Lectures on the History of Religions for which the American Council of Learned Societies, through its Committee on the History of Religions, assumed responsibility in 1936.

Under the program the Committee from time to time enlists the services of scholars to lecture in colleges, universities, and seminaries on topics in need of expert elucidation. Subsequently, when possible and appropriate, the Committee arranges for the publication of the lectures. Other volumes in the series are Martin P. Nilsson, *Greek Popular Religion* (1940), Henri Frankfort, *Ancient Egyptian Religion* (1948), Wingtsit Chan, *Religious Trends in Modern China* (1953), Joachim Wach, *The Comparative Study of Religions*, edited by Joseph M. Kitagawa (1958), R. M. Grant, *Gnosticism and Early Christianity* (1959), Robert Lawson Slater, *World Religions and World Community* (1963), Joseph M. Kitagawa, *Religion in Japanese History* (1966), Joseph L. Blau, *Modern Varieties of Judaism* (1966), Morton Smith, *Palestinian Parties and Politics That Shaped the Old Testament* (1971), Philip H. Ashby, *Modern Trends in Hinduism* (1974), Victor Turner and Edith Turner, *Image and Pilgrimage in Christian Culture* (1978), Annemarie Schimmel, *As Through a Veil: Mystical Poetry in Islam* (1982), and Peter Brown, *The Body and Society: Men, Women, and Sexual Renunciation in Early Christianity* (1988).

CONTENTS

vii

CONTENTS

ACKNOWLEDGMENTS

FIVE of these chapters were lectures prepared under the auspices of the American Council of Learned Societies. To the committee responsible for the invitation I express my grateful thanks for the honor which they did me. In particular I wish to thank Professor Willard G. Oxtoby for his interest and continuing support.

To these five have been added the essays which appear as chapters 1 and 4. Chapter 1 is a general lecture which I gave at various places in North America in 1986, slightly amended to bring it up to date. It was originally published in the *Harvard Divinity Bulletin* (January–May 1987) and I express my thanks to its editor, J. Michael West, for permission to reproduce it here. Chapter 4 is a paper which appears in a lengthier form in Joseph T. O'Connell, M. Israel, and W. G. Oxtoby, eds., *Sikh History and Religion in the Twentieth Century* (Toronto, 1988). I am grateful to my co-editors for permission to reprint it.

For their help on February 2, 1987, Ainslie Embree, Mark Juergensmeyer, and Jack Hawley earned gratitude I am unable to repay. I also acknowledge with profound thankfulness debts which I owe to Maureen Cafferty, J. P. Mohr, and James W. Correll.

To the many friends who helped my wife and me during our year in Toronto and in our travels around North America—Punjabis, Canadians, and others south of the border—I express my warmest thanks.

Finally, I am eternally grateful to Margaret for her never-failing love and support.

THE SIKHS

1

The Sikhs

EVERYONE, it seems, knows how to recognize a Sikh (or at least a Sikh man) and most people seem to have some notion of the general outlook and behavior to be expected of them. If a description of a Sikh is called for it will invariably focus on beards, turbans and possibly swords; a description of Sikh attitudes and behavior will probably have something to say about militant ideals and a willingness to perform violent deeds. And do they not want their own independent state in India? At this point the description begins to falter. We seem to have summarized everything that most people know about Sikhs.

Those who know the truth of the matter may well be offended by an introduction of this kind, believing that it can only serve to reinforce a most unfortunate and misleading stereotype. Many Sikh men do indeed wear beard and turban, but not all observe these conventions. Swords are seldom carried and acts of violence are confined to a very small minority; there is indeed a tradition of militancy within the Sikh community, but it is one which for loyal Sikhs is strictly controlled and legitimately expressed only under the most extreme circumstances. Just how many Sikhs support the demand for an independent state is debatable to say the least.

What we really need is a new and fairer stereotype. A just and accurate description of the Sikh community will certainly stress the common observance of a distinctive outward identity, but it will add that this convention is not practiced by all who call themselves Sikhs. It will recognize the presence of violence, but it will insist on limiting this feature to a tiny minority and it will maintain that Sikhs are no worse than other communities in this regard. It will also emphasize positive features which all too often are overlooked.

The usual way of correcting false impressions concerning the Sikhs is to offer a survey of the community's history. It is a sound method and it is the one which is adopted here, starting with the establishment of the community five hundred years ago.

The account begins with Guru Nanak, born into a Punjabi Hindu family in 1469. The life of Nanak is described with loving detail in traditional narratives (the janam-sakhis), but these need not detain us; they offer a hagiographic treatment which belongs to the piety of Nanak's later followers rather than to the reality of his actual life. Although they certainly exercise a considerable influence on Sikh perceptions of the first Guru, they must be set aside in favor of Nanak's own words.

The words of Nanak, preserved in the principal Sikh scripture (the Adi Granth), tell us little about his life but much about his doctrine and belief. The system of belief which lies behind the many hymns of Nanak begins by accepting the reality of karma and transmigration. All of us transmigrate in accordance with the deeds which we perform, and if we are to achieve liberation from the cycle of transmigration it is essential that we live the kind of life which will earn the requisite karma. Traditional teachings (both Hindu and Muslim) emphasize obedience to such outward conventions as temple or mosque worship, pilgrimage, the reading of sacred scriptures, and other such outward observances. Such practices are, according to Nanak, futile. Liberation can be achieved only by inward meditation directed to Akal Purakh, the "Timeless Being." True religion is interior.

Akal Purakh, as conceived by Guru Nanak, is the almighty Creator and Sustainer of the universe, without form and beyond human reason yet ever accessible to those who turn to him in true devotion. How can the seeker find him? Akal Purakh reveals himself in the *nām* or "divine Name," correctly understood as all that constitutes the divine reality. Because the entire creation is a part of the divine being, that same creation serves as the primary revelation of Akal Purakh. Akal Purakh is revealed in the world which lies about us and within us, and the world is thus to be understood as an expression of the *nām*.

In revealing himself through the *nām* Akal Purakh "speaks" the *śabad*, the divine Word which communicates the message of liberation to the devout believer. In so doing he acts as the eternal Guru. The eternal Guru is the mystical "voice" of Akal Purakh uttering the divine Word in the heart of the humble devotee: Open your eyes. Look around you and within you, for there you shall behold the divine harmony of the universe which Akal Purakh has created. Bring yourself into accord with that divine harmony and you will live the kind of life which earns you a liberating karma. Thus is eternal peace achieved and the cycle of transmigration brought to an end.

But how, in actual practice, can one achieve this harmony and live the kind of life which expresses it? Left to his own devices man follows the evil impulses which, dwelling within him, insistently prompt him to actions which can only prolong the cycle of rebirth. The solution lies in the practice of *nām simaran*, a regular discipline of inner meditation which focuses on the omnipresence of the divine Name.

The actual practice of *nām simaran* or "remembrance of the divine Name" ranges from the repeating of a word or mantra (one which summarily expresses the divine reality) to the singing of devotional songs and beyond that to mystical concentration of the most sophisticated kind. Each of these activities can be an effective method of *nām simaran*. The purpose is to bring the entire being of the devotee into harmony with the divine rhythm; and this is achieved through regular, disciplined remembrance of the divine Name by any or all of these methods. It requires no ritual observance, nor should the devotee abandon the world. The discipline is one which can be practiced by any man or woman in the customary circumstances of everyday life.

As the mediator of divine Name teachings Nanak acted as the "voice" of Akal Purakh. He acted, in other words, as the eternal Guru, and it is as Guru Nanak that he is characteristically known. During his life time he attracted disciples (the original Sikhs) and before he died he appointed a successor to follow him as the second Guru. Thus began the celebrated succession of the ten Sikh Gurus. Amidst continuing growth and varying circumstances the tradition lasted until the death of the tenth Guru, Gobind Singh, in 1708. By that time the community (or Panth as it is generally known) had undergone a dramatic change.

The dramatic change which was to transform the Panth did not take place in the time of the early Gurus. During the sixteenth century the Panth continued to develop, and this required a more structured organization as it matured and expanded. This included such important features as the founding of Amritsar as a sacred center, but until the beginning of the seventeenth century the Panth remains very much the Nanak-panth. It was the community of Nanak's followers, of those who revered the growing line of Gurus and accepted their teachings concerning deliverance through the divine Name. Although the fifth Guru, Arjan, implemented a decision of crucial significance by compiling a sacred scripture (the Adi Granth or Granth Sahib) the form and fundamental belief of the community remained unchanged. When Guru Arjan died in 1606 the Panth was still recognizably the Nanak-panth.

Guru Arjan's death was, however, highly significant in terms of future developments. The Mughal rulers of the Punjab had become suspicious of the growing community of Sikhs and Arjan's death in Mughal custody signaled the beginning of official hostility towards the Panth. This prompted an important change within the Panth. According to Sikh tradition Guru Arjan advised his son and successor Hargobind to sit fully armed on his throne; and Hargobind, as sixth Guru, symbolically donned two swords. Whereas one sword represented the continuing spiritual authority of the Guru (*pīrī*) the other signified a newly-assumed temporal authority (*mīrī*). Although there are some major problems associated with this tradition it is evident that the Panth was beginning to assume a new militancy and that it was doing this in response to the pressure of early seventeenth-century circumstances.

The new policy initiated by the sixth Guru climaxed with the dramatic actions of the tenth, Guru Gobind Singh. A period of relative peace had intervened during the middle decades of the seventeenth century, but under the Emperor Aurangzeb much stricter measures were adopted and in 1675 the ninth Guru was executed in Delhi. His son, acceding to the title of Guru as a child, was sheltered until he grew to manhood. As a young adult, however, he was soon involved in wars with hostile neighbors and eventually his enemies were joined by Mughal forces. Meanwhile he was evidently contemplating a major restructuring of the Panth and in 1699 he took the decisive step of summoning his followers to enter the newly established order of the Khalsa.

Those who heeded the Guru's summons and offered themselves for membership of the Khalsa were required to undergo a rite of baptism and to promise that thereafter they would accept the discipline required of all who were thus initiated. The baptismal water was stirred with a two-edged sword, and the discipline which all had to accept included certain exterior insignia which ensured that the male Sikh would thereafter be instantly recognizable. This much is clear and apparently beyond dispute. There are, however, several issues associated with the founding of the Khalsa which still raise difficulties and some of these are too important to ignore.

There is, for example, the question of precisely what the Guru aimed to achieve. Was he seeking to infuse a martial spirit by requiring all to accept a baptism which symbolically exalted the sword? Was he imposing an outward identity in order to ensure that Sikhs who had cravenly shrunk from recognition in the past would never again be able to conceal their identity? Or was he seeking to recall his Sikhs from loyalty to deputies (masand) who had once served the Guru faithfully but had now become independent and corrupt?

In summary terms it can be affirmed that an external identity became mandatory for the Sikh community (or at least for those Sikhs who elected to join the Khalsa) and two prominent features of that identity can also be affirmed. It certainly required all who accepted the Khalsa initiation to retain their hair uncut and bear arms. The newly-fashioned Khalsa community was thus a militant organization with an external identity which is typically perceived as the beard and the distinctive turban.

This much of the debate can be settled, but some of the other issues demand a little more attention. There are three such issues. First, how do we reconcile exterior symbols and explicit militancy with Guru Nanak's stress on inward devotion? Secondly, how is the militancy thus affirmed by the Khalsa ideal to be defined? Thirdly, did Guru Gobind Singh's decision mean that all Sikhs are required to become members of the Khalsa, or can one be a Sikh without actually observing the Khalsa discipline?

The first question arises from the fact that Nanak had preached interior meditation and had so plainly denounced all dependence on external practices as a means of spiritual deliverance. Yet what could be more obviously external than the conspicuous insignia of the Khalsa or indeed the greater part of the Rahit (the code of conduct) which its members are required to observe?

There are at least two answers to this apparent contradiction. The first is that all such communities eventually require at least a rudimentary organization and pattern of behavior. The original adherents of any such movement may live by the vision and depend exclusively on the power of personal conviction. For later generations and larger numbers, however, a more objective order is needed.

The second answer is that circumstances had changed. The first Sikhs to gather at Nanak's feet were closely united by their common allegiance and their existence generated no significant hostility. A century later, however, the Panth had become larger and more diverse. Conventions had been imported into the community by those who joined it, and its growing size had begun to cause alarm amongst the rulers. By the end of the seventeenth century internal pressures and external hostility had become serious and the policy adopted by the tenth Guru was bound to differ from that of the first.

To these two explanations Sikh tradition adds a significant gloss, an interpretation which derives directly from the doctrine of the eternal Guru. The eternal Guru is one and undivided. Proceeding from Akal Purakh it was mystically embodied in the ten Gurus, moving from each to his successor as a single flame passes from one torch to another. The Guru who instituted the Khalsa was thus the same Guru as he who had preached interior devotion to the divine Name, a single divine intelligence which must obliterate all possibility of inconsistency.

The second major question raised by the founding of the Khalsa concerns the nature of the militancy which its members are expected to practice. Does the Khalsa ideal encourage naked violence, strictly limited defensive postures, or something in between? The answer to this particular question has an obvious bearing on the current crisis in the Punjab. If a militant response is permitted or required then precisely how is that response to be defined?

Sikh tradition is clear on this point. Sayings attributed to Guru Gobind Singh certainly affirm the right to draw the sword, but they also add two major qualifications. The first is that the sword may be used only in defense of truth, of righteousness, and of the faith; and the second is that it may be drawn only when all other means of defense have failed. It is thus made clear that the sword may be wielded only to defend fundamental rights, and that it may be drawn only as a last resort. Needless to say, this still leaves open the definition of "fundamental rights," but at least it demonstrates that as far as the tradition is concerned there is absolutely no sanction for selfish, unprovoked or capricious use of violence. The tradition certainly affirms militancy as the proper response in certain circumstances, but they are circumstances which should seldom arise. Whether or not they have arisen in recent years is a question to which we shall return.

The third question posed by the inauguration of the Khalsa concerns its relationship to the Sikh Panth. Are the two coterminous? In other words, must all Sikhs be members of the Khalsa or is it possible to be a non-Khalsa Sikh? Is it possible to follow the teachings of Nanak without accepting a bounden duty to observe the later discipline of the Khalsa?

If we set the question in the context of Guru Gobind Singh's own time we shall soon discover that some of his leading disciples did not receive the Khalsa initiation. From this it presumably follows that one may indeed be a loyal Sikh without being a Sikh of the Khalsa. The Khalsa may well be perceived as the ideal or orthodox form, but historically there is insufficient basis for claiming that *all* Sikhs must be Khalsa Sikhs. The term which is used during the eighteenth century to designate the non-Khalsa Sikh is *Sahaj-dhārī*. This is set in contrast with *Amrit-dhārī*, the term which denotes a Sikh who has "taken *amrit*" (that is a Sikh who has received the baptism of the Khalsa).

To this preliminary judgment must be added the fact that there are actually more than two Sikh identities and that today there is increasing pressure to acknowledge only the Khalsa version as acceptable. In Sikh society today at least four definable identities can be distinguished. At either extreme stand the Amrit-dhari and the Sahaj-dhari. In between there are the *Kes-dhārī* and those who for want of a better term we must call the *Monā* Sikhs. The Kes-dhari Sikhs are those who maintain the uncut hair of the Khalsa, but do not receive baptism. The Mona Sikhs are those who cut their hair, but who are distinguished from the Sahaj-dhari by their connections with the Khalsa. This normally means that they belong to families with a Khalsa tradition and retain the Khalsa names (Singh for men and Kaur for women).

If Guru Gobind Singh had anticipated a period of conflict for his Sikhs he was certainly justified by the events of the eighteenth century. For the remainder of his life time he was repeatedly involved in warfare with neighboring states and with Mughal forces (the imperial power of the time), and the struggle continued well into the eighteenth century. The enemy changed as Mughal authority rapidly diminished and Afghan invaders took its place, but the hostility persisted with the Sikhs on one side and Muslim antagonists on the other.

This is the heroic period of Sikh tradition, the century which tested the Khalsa and proved it to be unyielding. It is also the period which critically molded the actual conventions of the Khalsa. By the time it emerged from that crucially important century its basic conventions were well defined. Khalsa Sikhs do not cut their hair, they do not touch tobacco, they wear distinctive blue garments, and they wield a skillful sword. They also emerged in triumph. The turn of the century marks the effective beginning of the reign of Ranjit Singh, Maharaja of a united Punjab until his death in 1839.

The death of Ranjit Singh was soon followed by political and military collapse. The British had been on his borders since early in his reign and following two brief wars with his successors the Punjab became a part of British India in 1849. Very soon the new rulers were confidently predicting the imminent demise of the Sikh faith, firm in their assurance that the Sikhs would "merge back into Hinduism."

We enter here upon another of the crucial periods in Sikh history, at once important for what it produced and uncertain in terms of how change actually took place. The clear result was eventually to be a reaffirmation of the Khalsa identity as the orthodox form for those who regarded themselves as Sikhs. 1873 traditionally marks the beginning of the period, for that was the year in which the first Singh Sabha was founded. Alarmed by evidence of wavering loyalties a group of Sikh leaders gathered in Amritsar and decided to establish a society dedicated to recovery and reform. Although the Singh Sabha movement was to be plagued by divisions, some of its more determined members nevertheless succeeded in generating a major restatement of the Sikh faith, and during their period of influence there was a strong move towards a restored Khalsa loyalty.

In this regard the British may also have played a part by favoring the Sikhs as one of the "martial races of India" and by requiring their Sikh recruits to observe the full regalia of the orthodox Khalsa identity. Army or police authorities who seek to discourage such conventions today might well ponder the British example. The British firmly encouraged such observances because they rightly believed that by maintaining them they would ensure higher morale and a stronger loyalty.

The Singh Sabha movement was overtaken during the second period of the present century by a more radical Sikh leadership, and during the period 1920–1925 the newly-formed Akali Dal (Akali Party) waged a non-violent struggle with the British authorities. The objective of the campaign was to have control of the principal gurdwaras (temples) transferred from their hereditary incumbents to the community as a whole. Needless to say, the episode was a great deal more complex than this would suggest and much remains to be learnt. Once again we must be content with a summary of the actual outcome.

The British, recognizing the strength and determination of the Akali movement, eventually agreed to vest control of the gurdwaras in a committee elected by adult Sikh suffrage. The committee assumed the name Shiromani Gurdwara Parbandhak Committee (or SGPC); and the all-important definition of the Sikh voter written into the 1925 Sikh Gurdwaras Act implied that such voters would be Khalsa Sikhs. This was not explicitly stated, merely the requirement that all should be Sikhs and only Sikhs. In effect this excluded a substantial proportion of the Sahaj-dharis, most of whom regarded themselves as both Hindu and Sikh. Khalsa Sikhs typically have no such sense of a dual identity.

The 1925 Act settled one issue, but political circumstances soon raised a more serious problem. As British India moved towards independence in the 1940s the prospect of partition became a real possibility. What would this mean for the Sikhs? One proposal would deliver their traditional homeland to the Muslim state of Pakistan, an option which Sikhs could never willingly accept. An alternative, scarcely more welcome, would have it divided between the two successor states. In the event it was the latter which occurred in 1947, driving the Sikhs (and the Hindus) of western Punjab across the new border into the eastern section retained by India.

Although Partition caused widespread chaos the Indian portion of the Punjab recovered with remarkable speed, at least in economic terms. The Punjab is an unusually fertile area and aided by new strains of wheat its cultivators were soon producing a rich return from their harvest. This brought prosperity to the fortunate few who owned land in sufficient quantity, and a substantial proportion of the beneficiaries were Sikhs. Those who gained most from the so-called "Green Revolution" were mainly Sikhs who belonged to the Jat caste. Jat Sikhs had long been both the dominant caste in rural Punjab and by far the largest caste group within the Sikh community. Inevitably the political developments which have occurred in modern Punjab conspicuously involve members of this particular sector of Punjabi society. Economic success was welcome, but it alone was not enough. There still remained the question of Sikh identity and the role of Sikhs in Punjabi society and government. Those who sought to protect and nourish the traditional Khalsa identity generally believed that for this purpose a well-disposed administration would be essential, one which would protect Sikh interests without penalizing other communities. This was the real motive which lay behind the campaign for Punjabi Suba (Punjabi State), though the ostensible cause was language.

The demand for Punjabi Suba required a state boundary which corresponded to the divide separating Punjabi and Hindi speakers, and this in practice meant a smaller state than the Punjab which took shape in India at independence. Prior to independence the Sikhs had formed the third-largest community in undivided Punjab. Partition had separated them from the Muslims, but even in the post-1947 Indian state they were still a minority. A redrawing of the boundaries on linguistic lines would finally produce a Sikh majority and with it the prospect of reasonable protection for Sikh interests.

Although the linguistic demand was strictly in accord with the provisions of the Indian constitution, Jawaharlal Nehru resisted it, regarding it as a covert form of communalism. Eventually it was his daughter Indira Gandhi who conceded the claim, partly in response to the notable contribution made by Sikhs during the Indo-Pakistan War of 1965. Punjabi Suba was granted in 1966 and for the first time since the collapse of Ranjit Singh's kingdom Sikhs could feel that they had a state of their own.

But the reality proved to be very different. The majority conferred by the redrawing of the state boundary was not a large one and it was immediately nullified by a division of Sikh support between the Akali Dal (which claimed to represent the distinctive interests of the Sikhs) and the Congress Party (which claimed to be strictly secular). Punjabi Suba certainly involved a much greater use of the Punjabi language for official purposes, and that was undoubtedly a gain, in that Sikhs have a strong affection for what they regard as their own special language. In other respects, however, there was little evidence to suggest that Punjabi Suba had made any significant difference to Punjabi society in general or to Sikh interests in particular.

Up to this point there are unlikely to be strong differences of opinion with regard to the unfolding pattern of Punjab politics or the role of Sikhs within that pattern. From here on, however, we enter disputed territory and it becomes necessary to present two conflicting interpretations. One of these interpretations is dominant in India as a whole and largely informs the presentation of news which emanates from New Delhi and the Punjab. It is, in other words, the perspective which one generally finds in the media, although there have been recent signs of a change in this regard. The other interpretation is the view which one may expect to hear within the Sikh community.

The dominant view runs, more or less, as follows: Having failed to secure their objectives by means of Punjabi Suba those who sought a distinctively Sikh state initiated a new campaign on two fronts. One objective was to secure a larger measure of state autonomy. The other was to rally Sikh support to the Akali Dal, thus ensuring that the larger autonomy could be utilized to protect Sikh interests. Whereas the former objective was promoted on the all-India stage the latter was pursued within the Punjab. Sikhs were to be persuaded that the Panth was in danger, and that only by loyalty to its traditions and its declared defenders could it be saved.

Amongst those who led the campaign (so this version continues) were many who could be described as "moderates," men and women who supported a limited increase in state autonomy and who wanted no part in violence. The objective and the rhetoric served, however, to raise up wilder men. These were the "extremists," a variety of Sikh dedicated to the simplistic notion of an independent Khalistan and more than willing to use brutal violence as a means to attain it. Bit by bit the threats and strong-arm tactics of the extremists weakened the resistance of the moderates while their inflamatory appeals to the martial traditions of the community won them increasing support from the rank and file. Under the fiercely malign leadership of Sant Jarnail Singh Bhindranwale the extremists entrenched themselves in the buildings surrounding the Golden Temple, eventually necessitating military action in early June 1984.

The attack on the Golden Temple complex succeeded in killing Bhindranwale and many of his followers, but the crisis was not yet over. Mrs. Gandhi's own bodyguard had been subverted by extremist propaganda with the result that she was assassinated by two of her guards on October 31, 1984. This killing, together with the many others which have since occurred in the Punjab and elsewhere, mean that the crisis is not yet over. There must be several years of firm resistance to unacceptable Sikh demands before peace and stability can eventually return to the Punjab. The alternative would be to risk the very unity of India, a possibility which no responsible citizen could contemplate.

That is one interpretation. The other one claims that the Punjab issue must be set within the context of all-India politics and specifically the electioneering strategy of the ruling Congress government in New Delhi. In order to maintain control of the central government the Congress Party must retain solid support in the dominant Hindi-speaking area of northern central India. This is best achieved by single-issue electoral campaigns based on incidents such as the Bangladesh War or on striking claims such as Mrs. Gandhi's famous slogan *Garībī haṭāo* (Abolish poverty). Congress strategists had decided that the issue for the mid-eighties should be the unity of India and that in order to promote this issue some potential threats to Indian unity should be given prominence. The areas which could conceivably serve this purpose were Assam, Kashmir and the Punjab. These three states could be represented as menacing the unity of India if strong Congress government were not retained.

In the case of the Punjab a part of this strategy involved the locating of a Sikh leader who, by the stridency of his demands, would simultaneously embarrass the Akalis and prove the point about threats to national unity. The person chosen for this purpose was none other than Jarnail Singh Bhindranwale, inducted into Punjab politics in accordance with Congress strategy.

Unfortunately Bhindranwale turned out to be more than merely strident. He proved to be his own man, eventually necessitating armed action on a scale not originally envisaged. This did not mean, however, that the strategy had failed. On the contrary, it was succeeding very well indeed. As reports of mounting violence circulated the rest of India took fright and increasingly rallied to the support of Congress. This support became overwhelming with the assassination of Mrs. Gandhi, sweeping her son Rajiv to the most impressive of all Congress victories.

With the electoral objective achieved Rajiv Gandhi could afford to be magnanimous and in July 1985 he reached an agreement with the "moderate" Sikh leader Sant Harchand Singh Longowal. This agreement conceded most of what the Akalis had all along been demanding, thereby raising the question of why the central government had previously offered such strenuous resistance. Elections were subsequently held in the Punjab and amidst general relief the Akalis won. The distasteful task of quelling the violence could now be left to the Sikhs themselves.

By now, however, a Pandora's box was well and truly open. Feelings had been violently inflamed and politicians in other parts of India had discovered the rewards to be secured by maintaining the Congress strategy. Rajiv Gandhi may have been sincere in signing the Punjab Accord of July 1985 but his control was insufficiently secure to enable him to deliver on his promises. The test case was his promise that the city of Chandigarh would be transferred from central government control to the Punjab on January 26, 1986. Two years later Chandigarh still remains untransferred.

The Sikhs have meanwhile been subjected to a concerted campaign ranging from vilification to murder. The latter reached a gory climax during the days immediately following the assassination of Mrs. Gandhi in killings which seemed plainly to reflect political planning and direction. To their suffering has been added a campaign of deliberate misinformation designed to convince India and the world that the root of the problem lay in Sikh intransigence and Sikh violence.

That is the other interpretation and time alone will tell which of the two is the more accurate. There are, however, some certainties to which we can point, the first concerning the claim that Sikhs must have their own independent state: the Punjab should be separated from India and reconstituted as the nation-state of Khalistan. Although no one can cite reliable figures or accurately estimate proportions, there seems to be little doubt that few Sikhs in India regard Khalistan as a realistic option. It should also be recognized, however, that the *notion* of Khalistan exercises a powerful appeal as far as Sikh sympathies are concerned. However impractical it may be it nevertheless provides an immediate focus for outraged feelings and for the anger of frustration.

The second point deserving emphasis is that the Sikh sense of outrage is entirely understandable, regardless of how one interprets the past and regardless of the solutions which one may envisage for the future. The attack on the Golden Temple complex had a traumatic effect on Sikhs everywhere, as did the killings which followed the assassination of Mrs. Gandhi. Repeated emphasis on Sikh violence and cases of calculated humiliation aggravate that sense of outrage, and the feeling is further strengthened by the repeated implications that violence is somehow confined to the Sikhs. Why, they insistently ask, does violence by others receive such little attention? Most such instances are, they maintain, ignored and the few which receive attention are typically represented as a provoked backlash.

This sense of outrage can be regarded as a general Sikh response, one which will be found amongst Sikhs of virtually all backgrounds and opinions. To it must be added as a third point the fact that two significant cleavages have developed within the Sikh community. To some extent the first and principle line of division follows the traditional boundary separating rural Sikhs from those who belong to urban castes. While strongly censuring government policy the latter nevertheless tend to distance themselves from the fiercer reactions of the rural community, and to talk in terms of compromise and settlement rather than retaliation or revenge. In the villages one encounters a stronger sense of grievance and a lesser willingness to seek conciliation.

Repeatedly one reads of or hears references to young village men who have disappeared, and to claims that these young Sikhs have been seized and killed. Here too it is impossible to obtain anything resembling accurate figures, but there can be little doubt that strong feelings have been generated by this issue and that they are feelings which will not easily dissipate.

Many young men from village families have become seriously disaffected and in the villages there appears to be widespread if covert support for their activities. The sympathy which they command is reflected in a devout remembrance of Jarnail Singh Bhindranwale and it ensures that they will usually be protected from the police. Their objectives may generate an uncertain response, they may lack firm leadership, and they may be ever vulnerable to factional splits, yet none of these problems spells an easy end to their disaffection. Their resistance continues and neither firmness nor conciliation, timely concessions nor government compromise hold promise of an effective solution.

The other divisive feature of particular concern derives from the ever-widening gap between Hindu and Sikh in the Punjab. In this, as in so many other respects, it is difficult to gauge the true nature or extent of alienation, but no one seems inclined to contest its existence. It is, indeed, an issue which extends well beyond the Punjab. In other parts of India Sikhs have reported a growing hostility, and the tendency for Hindus to move away from the Punjab is accompanied by a discreet movement of Sikhs in the opposite direction. The actual numbers seem not to be great, but many have taken the precaution of ensuring that they own property in the Punjab. Sikhs living in the Delhi area feel particularly insecure, well remembering the days and nights which followed the assassination of Mrs. Gandhi.

Our account of the Sikhs must remain unfinished. In a sense, of course, this is inevitable, for as long as there is life in a community or a people their narrative will continue to unfold. The record of the Sikhs is at a critical stage, however, and few observers would be prepared to predict it far into the future. Just what that record holds time alone will tell.

2

The Origins
of the Sikh Tradition

SIKHISM, we are often told, is a sect of Hinduism. Guru Nanak may have founded a new panth or religious community within the larger Hindu fold, but he neither violated nor abandoned the Hindu tradition. Born a Hindu, he remained one until the day he died, and so too did his successors. The doctrines which he affirmed were already current in the North India of his own period and the message which he preached was entirely congenial to many of his Hindu audience. Panths are a regular feature of the Hindu experience and Nanak, together with his followers, merely added one more. If we seek the origins of the Sikh tradition the place to look is surely the wider area of Hindu tradition and specifically the teachings of the Sants. Nanak did not found "Sikhism," for this would have meant founding something which already existed.

That is one point of view. A rather different version of the claim that Nanak did not found Sikhism has been expressed by Wilfred Cantwell Smith: "To call him "the founder of Sikhism," as is often done, is surely to misconstrue both him and history."[1] Professor Smith did not have contemporary Hindu doctrine or the Sant tradition in mind when he made this statement. He was looking forward to the "Sikhism" which we know today, insisting that his criticism of the common verdict on Nanak relates to the future implications of the term "Sikhism" rather than to the past. Sikhism, he maintains, is the evolved product of subsequent centuries, a complex system of beliefs and practices which Guru Nanak certainly did not "found." Nanak had "preached a vision." The organization and institutions came later (p. 67).

In many respects Cantwell Smith's analysis is an exceedingly helpful one, but does it not leave us where we started with regard to the origins of the Sikh tradition? If "Sikhism" is to be construed as a later development it must surely mean that both Nanak and the early Nanak-panth are to be located firmly within the Hindu tradition. Problems, however, persist and they are considerably aggravated by the claim that Sikhism (or the Nanak-panth) must be regarded as a sect of Hinduism. To Cantwell Smith's comment on "Sikhism" we can add his sensible insistence that there is no such thing as "Hinduism" (pp. 65–66). A sect, moreover, necessarily implies the existence of an agreed orthodoxy and even those who envisage an entity called Hinduism might well baulk at defining its orthodox form. The proposition that Sikhism is a sect of Hinduism is beginning to look distinctly unsatisfactory.

One must also be aware that the proposition will sound exceedingly offensive to many Sikhs. This cannot be lightly dismissed as a prejudice of the naive or the result of generations of biased nurture. Although Sikh scholars are certainly prepared to acknowledge the major developments that take place during the centuries following Nanak they are most unlikely to accept the notion that he merely replicated a range of doctrines and ideals current within the society of his own time.

Professor Harbans Singh, a distinguished interpreter of Sikh history and tradition, explicitly affirms that Guru Nanak was indeed the founder: "Attempts have been made to split Guru Nanak's doctrine into various strands and to trace their origin to preceding schools of thought. But to understand Guru Nanak fully, we have to look at the totality of his tenet and at what impact it made on history. In this perspective, we shall see that Guru Nanak is historically the founder of the Sikh faith. His precept was definitively the starting-point. In many significant ways, it signalled a new departure in contemporary religious ethos."[2] To ensure that his interpretation is clearly understood Harbans Singh quotes the words of the Indian Muslim scholar M. Mujeeb: "The revelation that came to Guru Nanak must have been direct and immediate and as independent of history and social circumstances as the religious records of the Sikhs show it to be."[3]

There is certainly an orthodox Sikh point of view concerning the status of Guru Nanak, and Harbans Singh expresses it soberly. Others state it with a vehemence. This plainly is their right and outsiders must learn to appreciate their view. It is a conspicuous feature of modern Sikhism and we might well conclude that its mere existence demolishes any claim that Sikhism can be sensibly regarded as a sect of Hinduism or of anything else.

But this acknowledgment does not solve the real problem. There are in fact several problems concerning Guru Nanak which still remain, and the historian cannot be deflected from a potentially embarrassing task by the strength of a modern interpretation or the vehemence of its supporters. The relationship of Nanak to the belief systems of his own day remains an issue, one which must be reexamined in some detail during the course of this chapter. The other problem which must also be reviewed arises from the traditional accounts of Nanak's life story and the treatment which these accounts receive today.

Although both problems were raised as long ago as 1968 in *Gurū Nānak and the Sikh Religion* it seems that both are still very much with us.[4] Quite by chance *Gurū Nānak and the Sikh Religion* appeared at an unusually fortunate time; indeed, it would have been necessary to wait 500 years for a better opportunity to publish such a book. It was first issued in November 1968 in anticipation of the year marking the quincentenary of the birth of Nanak. The reception which it was to receive was foreshadowed in the speech read by the Chief Justice of India at the principal United Kingdom function held to celebrate the quincentenary. Speaking in the Albert Hall in mid-1969 Mr. M. Hidayatullah delivered an address which comprised two distinct sections. The first portion dealt with the life of Nanak and for this section the speaker ignored *Gurū Nānak and the Sikh Religion*, relying instead on the janam-sakhis (the traditional narratives of the Guru's life[5]). In the second half, however, the tone of the speech changed dramatically. The second section dealt with the teachings of Nanak and it soon became clear that much of it had been drawn from *Gurū Nānak and the Sikh Religion*, some of it word for word.

This has since proved to be the standard response to the book. Whereas its treatment of the teachings of Nanak seems to have been largely accepted, its analysis of the biographical traditions has generally been ignored within the Panth. The one significant qualification attached to the teachings portion of the book has been its treatment of Guru Nanak's status as "founder" of the Sikh tradition. That issue will be discussed further following an examination of the response to the book's claim that the janam-sakhis are untrustworthy as records of the actual life of Guru Nanak.

The claim that the janam-sakhis are untrustworthy as biographical sources was not meant to suggest that they are valueless as historical records. They are indeed valuable in this regard, but their value principally derives from the insight which they supply concerning the developing beliefs of the later Panth. This issue was subsequently treated in *Early Sikh Tradition*,[6] a book which was written as a companion volume to *Gurū Nānak and the Sikh Religion*. The earlier work had focused on the janam-sakhi contribution to our knowledge of the actual details of the Guru's life; and the conclusion which it drew was that they provide very little reliable information. From this it followed that little could be known about the life of Guru Nanak, for apart from the janam-sakhis early references to Nanak are exceedingly scarce. His own considerable works, faithfully recorded in the Adi Granth, provide nothing more than an occasional glimpse, fleeting and tantalizing. The final conclusion was that the known life of Guru Nanak could be recorded in four short paragraphs.[7]

The first response to the biographical portion of *Gurū Nānak and the Sikh Religion* was a brief flurry of activity intended to probe its findings and to test them rigorously. Contemporary sources were scrutinized and scholars were despatched to Assam, Sri Lanka, and Baghdad. These are places which figure prominently in the traditional records and which had received special attention in the book's analysis.[8] The expedition to Sri Lanka produced new information which seemed, at first sight, to offer strong support for a visit by Guru Nanak. Subsequently, however, it was shown that information which had been supplied in Sri Lanka and accepted in good faith was in fact wholly inaccurate.[9] The effort to disprove the claims made in *Gurū Nānak and the Sikh Religion* thereafter lost its drive and little has been done since. A few books show that the biographical message of *Gurū Nānak and the Sikh Religion* has been understood and that their authors have generally accepted it.[10] For the most part, however, this portion of the book has been ignored.

Most publications from within the Panth thus continue to treat the janam-sakhis as acceptable sources for the life of Guru Nanak and to supply accounts based on the anecdotes which they record. There is, it is true, a rationalizing process at work in that the grosser elements are eliminated leaving only a refined product. It is nevertheless a very substantial remnant, one which offers a marked contrast to the four paragraphs in *Gurū Nānak and the Sikh Religion*. It is, moreover, a version which continues to bear the visible imprint of M. A. Macauliffe. Together with his Singh Sabha associates Macauliffe had decided that the *Purātan* janam-sakhi tradition supplied a more creditable account of the life of Nanak than the other available traditions.[11]

It was thus the *Purātan* schema which provided Macauliffe with his framework and ever since his work was published in 1909 it has dominated the field. Details continue to be drawn from the other janam-sakhi traditions, but the usual pattern remains the distinctive chronology and itinerary of the *Purātan* version. This follows the standard account as far as Nanak's childhood and early adulthood are concerned, but when it comes to the period of his travels it adopts a *dig-vijaya* perspective and sends him on journeys to the four cardinal points of the compass. The *Purātan* version offers a relatively coherent reordering of the many anecdotes which together constitute the janam-sakhis and it is not surprising that it should have exercised a strong appeal for men with an essentially rational approach to the problem of biography.[12]

In terms of its biographical analysis, therefore, *Gurū Nānak and the Sikh Religion* seems largely to have failed, at least within the Panth. This is unfortunate, for there are at least three reasons for concern. While these reasons need not mean that the specific findings of the book must be accepted in detail, if valid they will at least suggest that the time has come to review its general approach and to determine again whether or not that approach deserves to be reapplied. This task, if it is undertaken, should also involve a review of the case for janam-sakhi interpretation which is made in *Early Sikh Tradition*. The issue depends upon a thorough understanding of the nature and content of the janam-sakhis, aspects of the general problem which were not adequately covered in *Gurū Nānak and the Sikh Religion*.

The first reason concerns the relationship between the life of Guru Nanak and his many compositions recorded in the Adi Granth. Although it will sound exceedingly presumptuous it must nevertheless be maintained that these works cannot be fully understood if they are not set firmly within their historical context. A very significant portion of that context consists of the actual life of the Guru. It may not be possible to ascertain many of the details of that life, but we should at least protect ourselves against mistaken or misleading versions. Read literally the janam-sakhis must lead us into that trap. They are themselves interpretations of the life and mission of Baba Nanak, and if we trust them as historical records of the actual life of Guru Nanak they will assuredly skew our interpretation of his works.

A conspicuous example of this effect is supplied by the strong janam-sakhi insistence on the irenic purpose of the Guru's mission. "Nā koī hindū hai nā koī musalamān," he is alleged to have declared as he emerged from his life-changing vision of Akal Purakh: "There is neither Hindu nor Muslim."[13] In another famous *Purātan* reference Baba Nanak is said to have dressed in an odd assemblage of clothes combining Hindu and Muslim styles.[14] Other janam-sakhi features reinforce this image, leaving the clear and distinct impression that a fundamental intention of Guru Nanak's mission was to draw Hindu and Muslim together. There can be little doubt that this janam-sakhi image has significantly influenced the interpretation of Nanak's works. Indeed, it may well be the origin of the widespread yet erroneous notion that his works as a whole represent a conscious syncretism, one which sought to blend Hindu and Muslim beliefs. This notion, which will be discussed later, is an example of the risks associated with misconstruing the true nature of the janam-sakhis.

This leads to the second reason for disputing false interpretations of the janam-sakhis. It is not merely the life and work of Guru Nanak which must suffer from these misinterpretations; understanding of the janam-sakhis themselves will also suffer, and if they are to be treated as little more than sources for the life of Guru Nanak they will never yield their true value. The real value of the janam-sakhis concerns the later Panth.[15] Produced within the context of the developing Panth they can tell a great deal about it. The historian who seeks in them extensive material relating to the origins and growth of the Khalsa will be disappointed, but certainly not the scholar who works on the earlier period of development. Even the Khalsa period can be illuminated by a product such as the *B40 Janam-sākhī*[16] and because the janam-sakhis continue their growth right up to the recent past they can contribute insights across the entire span of Sikh history. This they are unlikely to

21

do if they are treated as documents and traditions relating exclusively to the actual life of Guru Nanak. Interpreted as biographies they are deprived of their true value.

A third reason for concern may perhaps be found in contemporary Sikh society, particularly those parts of it which constitute the modern Sikh diaspora in Western countries. The outsider who ventures to comment on Sikh society runs the risk of earning a well-merited rebuke, and the opinion which follows may well deserve this response. It does seem, however, that for those who value the religious content of the Sikh tradition there are considerable dangers associated with any insistence on treating the janam-sakhis as reliable records of the life of Guru Nanak.

Sikh children who receive a Western-style education will assuredly imbibe attitudes which encourage skepticism, and having done so they are most unlikely to view traditional janam-sakhi perceptions with approval. Given the emphasis which is typically laid on stories concerning Guru Nanak there is a risk that Sikhism as a whole may come to be associated with the kind of marvels and miracles which are the janam-sakhi stock-in-trade. Problems with this particular feature of the total Sikh tradition may well carry over into other areas. For some the price may be worth paying, but at least they should be aware of the risks involved in adopting the traditional approach. Seemingly harmless stories can be lethal to one's faith.

The janam-sakhi image of Baba Nanak leads us back to the problem with which we began and so to the Guru's teachings. There can be no doubt concerning the dominant janam-sakhi view of his status. From the wonders associated with his birth to the miraculous disappearance of his earthly body the stress is strongly on the divinity of Nanak and on the unique quality of his message. Here too the janam-sakhis have presumably exercised a significant influence on subsequent interpretations. Nurtured in this understanding of his role and status we can entertain only one possible view concerning the nature of his teachings. The message preached by Nanak was divinely given and unique, the Word of the eternal Guru uttered through its living embodiment. If this is indeed the case it presumably follows that the message began with Guru Nanak and that he is indeed the founder of the Sikh faith.

In spite of the sceptical tone running through this discussion there is an obvious case to be made for accepting the claim that Guru Nanak should be regarded as the founder of the Sikh Panth, and that in a certain sense the Panth can be construed as coterminous with the Sikh faith. There can be no questioning the fact that Guru Nanak attracted a group of followers; that these first disciples constituted the original nucleus of the Nanak-panth; and that the continuity of this newly-formed community was ensured by the appointment of a successor Guru and a spiritual lineage. If we are talking about the Panth, the line which we trace back in time must end with the person of Nanak, thus confirming his status as founder. The Sikh faith, however it may be conceived, is inextricably bound to the Panth and whatever influences may have molded the evolving Panth its connection with Nanak must surely be secure.

This, however, is avoiding the difficult issue associated with the general question of Sikh origins. Can the teachings of Nanak really be regarded as unique? The question leads us back to the claim with which this discussion began. It is a question which must be asked because the fundamental doctrines which inform the works of Nanak are to be found elsewhere in the North India of his own time and the immediate past. Here the reference is to the Sant tradition of North India, the range of religious understanding which stressed such features as the formless quality of God (*nirguna*) and a doctrine of deliverance which attached no significance to caste. This is the tradition which evokes such names as Kabir and Raidas. Outside the Panth most scholars include Nanak within the same tradition. Although the first Guru is seldom if ever called Sant Nanak (a title which most Sikhs would find exceedingly demeaning) his place within the movement is explicitly affirmed.

Nanak, it is claimed, replicated teachings which were already current in North India. Whether or not he received his doctrines from Kabir is of no consequence. The belief system promulgated by the Sants was gaining widespread currency and Nanak could have absorbed its ideals from a variety of possible sources. The fact that he so faithfully reproduces these doctrines sets him firmly within the Sant tradition, effectively destroying any claims to significant originality. Even the appointing of a successor does nothing to affect this judgment. Spiritual lineages are forever appearing and if one wants more recent examples with Sikh affiliations, the Nirankari, Namdhari, and Beas Radhasoami movements will readily oblige.

In stating the issue so frankly one runs a serious risk of causing grave offense and of alienating many readers before the real discussion has begun. It must nevertheless be clearly stated if we are to grapple adequately and sympathetically with the question of Sikh origins. Was

Nanak merely another Sant, or are there distinctive claims which may be entered on his behalf? If we concede that the links with Sant doctrine are altogether too obvious to be ignored must we then accept that the Sikh movement is a Sant movement? Should the Nanak-panth be properly regarded as one amongst many such panths emerging within the larger context of Hindu tradition and still remaining a part of it?

For some participants in this debate these questions normally imply affirmative answers, and the answers are commonly carried through to the present day. Subsequent developments may have transformed the later Panth, but it has never renounced its direct descent from the teachings of Nanak nor have its members effectively abandoned their place within the structure of caste society. For all participants the questions are not simply academic. They recur repeatedly within Sikh society and such incidents as the current crisis in the Punjab greatly sharpen their thrust.

In order to attempt an answer one must first understand the tradition which allegedly supplies the principal components of Nanak's doctrine; then survey the teachings of Nanak, briefly examining the fundamental features which they offer and setting those features within the total system which his works enable us to construct; and finally return to the problem of origins just broached and endeavor to find a solution.

The Sant tradition of northern India can be viewed both as a *sādhan* or method of spiritual liberation and as a form of social protest. Both elements are in fact inextricably linked. Most of the tradition's leading exponents were from lower castes and the theory of spiritual release which they state or assume in their religious songs is one which plainly rejects the relevance of caste status in matters pertaining to the soul's deliverance from the bondage of transmigration. Brahmans are typically scorned, as are all who claim to exercise authority as purveyors of religious merit or as mediators of divine grace. The condemnation was one which the Sants applied to all such authority and its claimants, Muslim as well as Hindu.

As this verdict makes clear the Sants laid firm and unqualified emphasis on the interior nature of the spiritual understanding and on the discipline required in order to secure freedom from the suffering of death and rebirth. Their ultimate goal remained the same as that of the Vaishnava bhakti with which Sant docrine has so often been confused, the same indeed as Hindu *sādhan* in general. The objective was *mokṣa*, liberation from the transmigratory cycle and from the suffering which necessarily attends it. There is no denying the reality of karma, nor of the consequences which ineluctably follow the actions which each individual performs. The difference concerns the method whereby one breaks or terminates the cycle and to some extent the quality of *mokṣa* which the Sants offered to all who followed their devotional discipline. This discipline was emphatically and exclusively interior, at least as preached by the more significant of the Sants. The objective was a permanent stilling of all emotion and all conflict, peace in an eternal equipoise which could be achieved by the devout Sant while still living out his present existence.[17]

From this brief summary it will be evident that the message preached by the Sants in their religious songs bears obvious resemblances to other traditions familiar in the North Indian experience. It is easy to see why they should have been confused with contemporary Vaishnava bhaktas, for both share the same uncompromising insistence on devotion as the way of liberation. The connection is, moreover, a legitimate one to the extent that the Sant tradition plainly derived fundamental features of its doctrine from Vaishnava belief. The Sant emphasis on interiority points to the other principal source of its belief and practice. This was the Nath panth, a contemporary representative of the ancient tantric tradition. Sufi influence may also have contributed to the development of Sant doctrine, though if this is indeed the case its results are much harder to detect in the terminology of the Sant than features which derive from Vaishnava and Nath sources.

Of these three contributors to Sant doctrine the least familiar is undoubtedly the Nath tradition.[18] Today it survives as a fading memory rather than as an active system with acknowledged leaders and dedicated practitioners of its yogic theory. During the time of Guru Nanak, however, it commanded a considerable influence in the Punjab and North India generally. Although its origins remain unclear there can be no doubt that they relate intimately to Shaivite teachings and to tantric Buddhism. The word *nāth* means "master" and the *Ādināth* or "Primal Nath" was identified as Shiva. In addition to the Adinath there were believed to exist nine other Naths, master yogis who had attained immortality through the practice of hatha-yoga and who were supposed to be living far back in the Himalayas. Of these nine the principal figure was, by common consent, the semi-legendary Gorakhnath to whom all adherents of the Nath tradition owed allegiance. Belief in the nine immortal Naths is obviously connected in some way with the eighty-four immortal Siddhas of tantric Buddhism. In Sikh tradition the two terms, Nath and Siddha, are used interchangeably with a strong preference attaching to the latter.

Adherents of the Nath tradition were commonly known as Kanphat or "split-ear" yogis, a name which derives from their practice of wearing large ear-rings. Their direct influence on the educated seems to have been limited, but amongst the people at large they evidently commanded respect for their austerities and aroused considerable dread for the magical powers which they were believed to possess. The songs attributed to Kabir are shot through with Nath concepts and terminology, clearly demonstrating the extent of their influence on a major representative of the Sant tradition. If these songs are the work of a single person called Kabir that person (regardless of his Muslim name) must surely have had close personal connections with the Naths. If they are to be regarded as the composite and evolved products of a Kabirian tradition the tradition itself was presumably subjected to a strong Nath influence. Whatever the root, Nath influences are plainly evident in the works attributed to Kabir and in other products of the Sant tradition. They are also present in the works of Guru Nanak.

The impact of this Nath influence can presumably be observed in the characteristic Sant stress on the irrelevance of caste status as a means to deliverance, the folly of sacred languages and scriptures, the futility of temple worship and pilgrimage, and their general stress on interior devotion. Such features are the essence of Sant belief. Their starting point is a concept of God which insists upon his wholly formless quality. He is *nirguṇa*, as opposed to the *saguṇa* belief which envisages physical incarnations and accepts visible representations in the form of idols. For the Sants all such exterior forms are misguided, as are the associated practices of temple worship and outward ceremony. God is to be found within each human heart or spirit, and there alone can one practice the loving devotion which will ultimately lead to union with the divine and thus to the eternal bliss of deliverance. The inner path which the devout Sant must follow is not an easy one, but its reward is sure and it is one which can be secured in this present existence. The reward is the bliss of total peace in mystical union. This is the condition of *sahaj*, a word which leads us back to the Naths and beyond them to the earlier tradition of tantric Buddhism.

This stress on Nath antecedents should not imply that the Sants were mere imitators of Nath belief and practice. Such a conclusion would be far from the truth, for the Sants were generally strong critics of the Naths, and their doctrine offers much more than Nath borrowings. *Sahaj*, they insist, is not to be attained through the practice of hatha-yoga. It is to be attained through inward devotion and the practice of meditation. In looking for the closest relatives of the Sants one must still acknowledge them to be the Vaishnava bhaktas, for the essence of Sant belief remains loving devotion to a personal deity. The points which must be repeatedly stressed are that the object of their devotion is a strictly formless God, and that the actual practice of devotion is a strictly inward discipline.[19]

An outline of Guru Nanak's system will show how closely its fundamental features match the insistent emphases of the Sant. The teachings of Nanak are easily accessible. Although his approach to the all-important question of spiritual deliverance is not that of a systematic theologian there can be no doubt that a developed and integrated system was present in his mind and that it informs the many hymns which he has left. The hymns were recorded in the Adi Granth half a century after his death and it appears that Guru Arjan, in compiling the Adi Granth, had access to an earlier collection compiled by the third Guru.[20] The source is thus a sound one and exegesis will reveal that a coherent system lies behind the hymns which it preserves.

In the earlier brief survey of Sant origins it was noted that Sufi doctrine may have exercised a limited influence on its development. In the case of Guru Nanak one commonly encounters the insistent claim that he owed much to Islam and specifically to the Sufis. As was also indicated, some writers have carried this theory to the point of claiming that his religion can be treated as an example of conscious syncretism, one which deliberately tried to blend Hindu and Muslim ideals. These interpretations were criticized in *Gurū Nānak and the Sikh Religion* where it was suggested that whatever Muslim influence might be detected in Nanak's work no aspect of that influence could claim fundamental significance.[21] This denial of the syncretism thesis was itself attacked and it must be acknowledged that were the book to be rewritten some marginal qualifications would be needed. The substance of the denial has, however, been confirmed by a much more thorough analysis of the issue, one which approaches it by way of the Persian loan-words which appear in the Adi Granth. The analysis is the work of Professor Christopher Shackle and the publication of his finds seems clearly to have demolished the old syncretic claim.[22]

Guru Nanak viewed both the Hindu tradition and Islam in a typically Sant manner. In their conventional forms both offered systems of belief and practice which largely relied on external authorities and outward response. As such both were to be condemned. Only those who perceived the inner reality of truth could achieve deliverance, and this end could be attained regardless of whether one were a Hindu or a Muslim. Those who followed this inner path are the "true" Hindu and the "true" Muslim as opposed to the "false" believers who continue to put their trust in ritual and pilgrimage, temple and mosque, brahman and mullah, Shastras and Qur'an.

As Professor Shackle demonstrates, the Islamic loan-words which appear in the works of Guru Nanak (as elsewhere in the Adi Granth) are normally used to express such themes as the "true" and the "false" Muslim. The most famous example occurs in a shalok from *Vār Mājh*.

> Make mercy your mosque and devotion your prayer mat,
>   righteousness your Qur'an;
> Meekness your circumcising, goodness your fasting,
>   for thus the true Muslim expresses his faith.
> Make good works your Ka'bah, take truth as your pir
>   compassion your creed and your prayer.
> Let service to God be the beads which you tell
>   and God will exalt you to glory.[23]

This is the classic Guru Nanak approach, typical both in terms of its insistent interior emphasis and of its striking use of imagery. In this particular instance it supplies a definition of the "true" Muslim and in so doing it illustrates the use which Nanak typically makes of Muslim concepts. The same contrast between the true believer and the false explains the conjoining of Hindu and Muslim names for God, and when Muslim names for God are elsewhere introduced it is commonly for the poetic purpose of achieving assonance or alliteration. The use of Islamic terms certainly does not guarantee an Islamic content.[24] Having noted this feature Professor Shackle adds (pp. 93–94): "Nor is this awareness of Islam, which is indeed evidenced by this and other uses of Islamic loan-words in the A[di] G[ranth], to be confused with any direct influence from Islam, as suggested by the proponents of the syncretic or eclectic origin of Sikhism, necessarily on the basis of secondary sources, since the primary text has so little to offer them by way of support."

Professor Shackle concludes his analysis by drawing attention to the fact that the Adi Granth borrowings from Persian concentrate much more heavily on images of royal authority than on the doctrines and practice of Islam (pp. 94–96). He adds that the relevant features present in the works of Guru Nanak are also to be found in those attributed to Kabir.

This analysis of Adi Granth terminology should make it possible to put aside, once and for all, the mistaken notion that Guru Nanak offers a synthesis of Hindu and Muslim ideals. The view that the Sant pattern of belief draws little of significance from Islam also bears repeating. The controversy is now becoming sterile, deserving to be briefly examined only because it still dominates popular representations of the teachings of Guru Nanak. For journalists covering the recent troubles in the Punjab it seems to have been a mandatory introduction for whatever they might say about Nanak and his influence.

Having thus discarded a mistaken interpretation of the teachings of Guru Nanak it is possible to proceed to a summary of what they actually contain, beginning, as the Adi Granth itself begins, with Nanak's doctrine of God. Many terms, drawn from a variety of traditions, are used to designate the God of Nanak's theology, each of them offering a facet of his total understanding. One which has achieved particular popularity is Akal Purakh, the "Person beyond Time" or "Eternal One." As one might expect from the Sant background of Nanak's thought Akal Purakh is understood as Nirankār, "the One without Form," and repeated emphasis is laid on the ineffable quality of his being. This does not mean, however, that Akal Purakh is inaccessible to the understanding of men and women or that he is beyond the reach of their affections. Akal Purakh has in fact manifested himself in the world which he has created, and they whose eyes are opened to spiritual understanding will perceive him immanent in all creation. Thus perceiving him they receive the means to approach him and so to appropriate the freedom and eternal bliss which is proffered for all to grasp.

Mankind, however, is congenitally blind and for most people the vision of the divine, ever present around them, remains forever concealed. The problem lies in the human man[25], that inner faculty which commonly we call our "heart" but which is better understood as a complex comprising heart, mind and spirit. Within the man evil exercises its vicious way and, seduced by the passions which it generates, most are blind to the spiritual reality which lies within and about them. Driven by their evil impulses they behave in a manner which, in accordance with the law of karma, earns appropriate penalties. For such people the result can only be the round of death and rebirth, the endless sequence which extends suffering through all eternity. The fundamental problem is *haumai* or self-centered concern for all that attracts the proud, the sensual and the selfish. As long as the *man* is in the grip of *haumai* there can be no hope of escape. The endless round must continue.

What, then, is the solution? The solution, according to Nanak, is the *nām* or the "divine Name." He who learns how to appropriate the *nām* will be freed from the chains which bind him to the wheel of transmigration. The term *nām*, as used by Nanak and elsewhere in Sant literature, is a summary expression for the whole nature of God and all that constitutes his being. It is, to use another favored expression, *sat* or "truth" and one commonly encounters the combination *satinām* or "True Name." Anything that may be affirmed concerning Akal Purakh constitutes an aspect of the divine Name, and a sufficient understanding of the divine Name provides the essential means to deliverance.

How is the divine Name to be appropriated? In what manner is it revealed and what must a person do in order to secure the reward which it confers? A knowledge of the Name can be attained because Akal Purakh is a God of grace, speaking the Word of divine understanding to all who are prepared to shed their *haumai* and listen in humility. The Word (*śabad*) is the message inscribed in creation, and the mystical "voice" whereby it is "spoken" is the eternal Guru. Akal Purakh is himself the eternal Guru, speaking through the creation which constitutes his visible form. The message thus spoken is the Word which reveals the divine Name. It is a simple message. Look around you and look within. Both around and within you will perceive the divine Order (*hukam*), a harmony expressed in the physical and psychical creation which reflects the divine harmony of Akal Purakh himself.

In order to secure liberation one must attune one's whole life to that harmony expressed as the divine Name. This purpose one achieves by means of regular, disciplined practice of *nām simaraṇ* or "remembrance of the Name." A simple version of this technique consists of repeating a word or expression which summarizes the meaning of the divine Name and thus of Akal Purakh himself (a word such as *satinām* or the later term *Vāhigurū*). The more sophisticated version is a technique of meditation which inwardly reflects upon the meaning of the divine Name, with the intention of bringing one's whole being into harmony with the divine harmony of the Name. *Kīrtan* (the singing of appropriate hymns) is another form of *nām simaraṇ*, for in this manner also devout believers can attune themselves to the divine.

The discipline is not an easy task, nor can one expect to secure the ultimate reward without lengthy striving. It is, however, a sure reward for those who sincerely seek it. All who follow the discipline of *nām simaraṇ* with devout persistence will progressively ascend to levels of spiritual experience which they alone can comprehend. The end is mystical union in the eternal bliss of total serenity. Thus is the cycle of transmigration broken. Thus does one merge in the divine Name.

Those who know the works attributed to Kabir and other Sants will find in this brief summary of Nanak's theology much that is familiar and nothing that conflicts with any significant feature of Sant doctrine. In Nanak, as in Kabir, there is the same rejection of exterior forms, the same insistence on the need for inward devotion and its sufficiency as the sole means of liberation.[26] We return to the problem which has recurred throughout this survey of the life and teachings of Guru Nanak. Must we conclude that Nanak was a Sant?

The answer will depend on the tone and color of the question. If it is a strictly neutral question of antecedents and influences the answer must be in the affirmative. Because he represents the essential concerns of the Sants we are bound to locate Guru Nanak within the Sant tradition. If, however, the question implies a lack of originality on the part of Nanak the answer must be an emphatic negative. Plainly there is much that is profoundly original in the hymns which we find recorded under his distinctive symbol in the Adi Granth.[27] There is in them an integrated and coherent system which no other Sant has produced; there is a clarity which no other Sant has equaled; and there is a beauty which no other Sant has matched. There is, moreover, the question of permanence. The fact that Nanak appointed a successor to follow him is scarcely unique, but nothing in the Sant experience can compare to the Panth which was eventually to emerge from that decision.

3

Four Centuries
of Sikh History

S URVEYING Sikh history since Nanak's death might seem to be an easy task. It would indeed be easy if it were possible to agree on the facts which should be presented, and upon their interpretation. In the case of Guru Nanak there should be no serious problem, at least as far as the facts are concerned. Whereas knowledge of his actual life must necessarily remain limited his teachings are readily accessible. As we have already seen there is a continuing controversy regarding the relationship of Nanak to the Sant tradition, but at least there should be little argument concerning either the paucity of biographical detail or the abundance of authentic compositions. Moving beyond his death in 1539, however, the task becomes much more complicated. Serious problems arise throughout the survey and any general interpretation that may be offered is bound to be disputed.[1]

One of these problems was indicated earlier when dealing with the life and teachings of Nanak. I trod then on sacred ground and must continue to do so. This means that an attitude of sympathetic caution must be sustained in order to hold the attention of a representative audience. The subject concerns the substance of a living faith, one which generates strong devotion and a fierce loyalty. It is not an area to be entered carelessly or with any hint of disrespect.

A second problem arises, as one might expect, from the restricted quantity of source material, notably with regard to the period preceding the nineteenth century. This is scarcely an issue peculiar to Sikh history. Other regional historians of India typically encounter the same problem, particularly if they must move away from official sources in order to obtain the material which they need. In the case of the Sikhs it has been reasonably argued that those who were making history during the eighteenth century were unaccustomed by tradition to recording it and far too busy to bother anyway. The increasingly disturbed conditions which encouraged this response would also have been responsible for the destruction of some portion of the small legacy. Whatever the reason, it is immediately obvious that sources which predate the nineteenth century are restricted in quantity and in coverage. A time of relative plenty is only reached with the nineteenth-century source materials (both Sikh and British).

The increase in supply which comes with the modern period certainly helps, but it does not solve all problems relating to sources. Whether these sources be scanty or profuse, whether of the sixteenth century or the late twentieth, there remains the general problem of how to interpret those sources. This has already been noted with regard to the janam-sakhis, the traditional narratives of the life of Nanak. Any response seems possible, from the wholly credulous to the totally sceptical. In practice the significant debate sets the cautiously traditional scholar against those trained in modern Western historiography. The difference of approach is one to which we shall return.

Moving from janam-sakhi interpretation into eighteenth-century materials a similar range of differing views is encountered with regard to the rahit-namas and the gur-bilas literature.[2] The early rahit-namas, which record various versions of the Khalsa code of conduct, invariably purport to date from the time of Guru Gobind Singh (1675–1708) or at least to report words which the author claims to have heard directly from his lips. These claims may be believed or they may be questioned. The response which each of us chooses must make a substantial difference both to the facts which we accept and to the interpretations which we derive from them.

The issue raised by the rahit-namas recurs when we turn to the gur-bilas literature, stirring accounts of the mighty deeds of the Gurus. These works typically concentrate on the life and mission of the tenth Guru, exalting both his wisdom and his steadfast heroism. In thus describing the gur-bilas literature one can immediately sense the presence of the first problem. It is very easy to sound critical or condescending, and if this be the result of such descriptions they can be very damaging indeed. Yet the point must be made and attention must be insistently drawn to the way in which these narratives are actually used. Too often they are cited as proof-texts for a cherished tradition without adequate scrutiny of their actual dates or of the purpose which they were intended to serve. Even those who are free from prior commitment or preconceived interpretation can fall into the trap. An example of that trap is provided by Koer Singh's *Gur-bilās Pātaśāhī 10*, a work which claims to be eighteenth-century in origin. *Gur-bilās Pātaśāhī 10* evidently belongs to the early nineteenth century and it serves a patently inspirational purpose.[3]

I shall return to these codes and narratives in chapters 5 and 6. They are cited here as important examples of the available sources for the middle period of Sikh history and of the differing responses which such materials can elicit. It should also be noted that this particular problem is not confined to Punjabi sources: Macauliffe's enormously influential *The Sikh Religion* must be intimately associated with the traditional approach, both with regard to its source-material value and as a trap for unwary researchers. Published in 1909 this six-volume study relies largely on traditional works, selectively organizing their material in a manner which answers the needs of consistency rather than those of critical scholarship. Macauliffe's work is justly renowned, but it should not be used as a reliable source except for the student of the Singh Sabha reform movement. The Singh Sabha movement developed within the Sikh community late in the nineteenth century, extending its active period of publishing and education into the early decades of the twentieth. From it Macauliffe drew much of his inspiration, and its ideals are faithfully reflected in his work.

Macauliffe's reputation leads to yet another of the serious problems confronting the student of Sikh history, one which was implied in my brief treatment of the sources issue. This final problem can be described as the burden of tradition. There are in fact two dominant traditions not merely the variety which so readily springs to mind; and, as we shall see, they produce two conflicting types of interpretation.

The obvious variety is that which preserves and presents a traditional view of Sikh history from within the Panth. This is indeed a major aspect of the problem. Scholars who have been nurtured in the Sikh tradition will naturally find it very difficult to comprehend with sympathy findings or interpretations which seriously contest a traditional view. This view, it should be noted, is one which essentially derives from the Singh Sabha reinterpretation of Sikh history. As such it draws extensively on traditional sources, interpreting them in an essentially conservative mode, and any approach to Sikh history which seems to be calling either the sources or the reinterpretation into question will be strongly resisted. The historiography and hermeneutics generated during the Singh Sabha period are still dominant and this inevitably means that a vigorous contest awaits the historian or theologian who challenges its approach.

This is one of the traditions which presents a problem. The other is the Western academic tradition with its strongly skeptical tone. Proponents of the first view assume that they have taken the measure of this one, for those who affirm the Singh Sabha approach will usually claim to have absorbed the benefits offered by Western historiography while discarding its excessive rationalism and rather absurd rigor. How can one possibly hope to understand the essence of the Sikh tradition if one lacks a sympathetic willingness to accept its definitions? And why should one refuse to acknowledge all but the definitively proven? The field must remain arid if this be the theory and the style.

The rebuke is a just one, for there can be no doubt that rigor and scepticism can be overdone. That admission does not mean, however, that the principles of rigor and scepticism should be abandoned. What is to be expected is that here, as in the scholarly study of any religious tradition, both approaches will continue to be evident and that a measure of scholarly tension is thus bound to persist. This tension need not involve fierce dispute or denunciation. On the contrary, it can be a generally creative tension and the proponents of either approach are exceedingly foolish if they refuse to listen sympathetically to the other.

Although the debate between the two sides affects many of the issues raised by a study of Sikh history one such issue commands a particular importance. This is the "transformation of Sikhism" theme. The question of why a tradition built on Nanak's interior practice of *nām simaraṇ* (meditation on the divine Name) should have become a militant community and proclaimed its identity by means of prominently-displayed exterior symbols. How, in Khushwant Singh's words, do we explain the transition "from the pacifist Sikh to the militant Khalsa?"[4]

There are actually two distinct issues involved in this general question. First, why did a religion of interiority assume such an overtly exterior identity? Secondly, why did the Panth adopt a militant philosophy and develop an appropriately militant tradition? The two issues deserve to be treated together, for they are intimately related in practice and the answers which are given to one set of questions must largely dictate the response to the other. Together they raise a fundamental question with a significance extending far beyond the bounds of academic debate. Differing answers to the fundamental question reflect differing responses to major issues which continue to agitate the Panth.

For some the fundamental question is posed in the following form: "Should the transformation have occurred?" Thus expressed the question commonly implies a negative answer, an answer which many Indians (including many Punjabi Hindus) are strongly inclined to support. The radical argument runs as follows: Nanak conferred great benefit on his own and succeeding generations by preaching the way of deliverance through the practice of *nām simaraṇ;* this is where Gurmat began and that is how it should have remained;[5] the later Gurus may well have been sorely provoked by Mughal authorities, but the decision to arm their followers and to redirect their teachings along militant lines was wholly regrettable. Religion should follow the path of peace, not the path of war.

A modified version of the argument accepts that there may have been reasons for the creation of the militant Khalsa order while firmly rejecting the claim that this should necessarily have transformed the Panth as a whole. The Khalsa should exist as a voluntary association within the larger Panth, to be joined by those who find value in its discipline but certainly not to exclude from the Panth others who prefer to limit their loyalties to the teachings enunciated by Nanak and his early successors. The divine Name teachings of Nanak should be regarded as the essence of Gurmat. The Khalsa mode should be treated as a strictly voluntary extra.

The modified version of the argument raises the difficult question of how one should regard those who affirm veneration for Nanak while rejecting the discipline of the Khalsa. I shall return to this question in Chapter 5, when seeking to define the nature of Sikh identity more precisely. At this point it can be acknowledged that Khalsa doctrine is strongly predominant within the Panth and that for all who accept the Khalsa tradition the question of its necessity simply does not arise. The historian who stands outside the Panth can likewise (for somewhat different reasons) set the question aside. There can be no doubt that a significant change did remodel the Panth and the relevant question must therefore be why this happened.

Four distinct answers have been given to this question, two of which should be scrutinized before we finally proceed to our summary survey of Sikh history. The other two theories are first that militancy was for the defense of the Panth; and second, a theory which can be summarily discarded, that credit for Sikh militancy must be bestowed on the nineteenth-century British rulers of the recent-annexed Punjab and on elite groups within the Panth itself who subsequently turned the same tradition against its creators. According to this latter interpretation there were several Sikh identities available during the period immediately following the 1849 annexation and one such identity (the militant Khalsa version) was vigorously promoted by the British in order to serve their own military purposes. The same identity was accepted by the stronger of the Singh Sabha leaders and became the focus of their reforming activities late in the nineteenth century.

A brief summary of this theory necessarily does it serious injustice and before passing on it should be acknowledged that it incorporates important insights for discussion later in this chapter.[6] In general terms, however, it can be rejected. It focuses much too narrowly on the condition of the Panth during the mid-nineteenth century, failing to take adequate account of the rise to dominance of the Khalsa ideal during the course of the eighteenth century.

The second answer which may be briefly covered, one with roots in early Sikh tradition, is that Sikh militancy was for the defense of the Panth. Because Nanak and his successors attracted an expanding group of followers the Mughal authorities in Delhi and Lahore became alarmed. Egged on by bigoted Muslims and a few malicious Hindus they began to take steps to suppress the movement. Confronted by this threat the later Gurus had little choice but to arm their followers or face extinction. They chose the former alternative, thereby converting the Panth from a group of unarmed devotees into one which was able to defend itself. This alone proved to be inadequate and eventually the firm discipline of the Khalsa had to be imposed on men who, in times of real danger, proved to be less than totally loyal.

This second theory can be treated summarily, not because it deserves to be rejected but because it is generally incorporated in the remaining theories. Neither of the two remaining theories accepts it as a sufficient answer to the transformation question, but they do accept that it is part of the total explanation. For both it is a subordinate aspect of the answer, a significant feature which should not be regarded as the core explanation.

There remain two conflicting interpretations, one of which has long dominated Sikh historiography and still shows little sign of weakening. This theory affirms that the Panth was remolded by Guru Gobind Singh in order to defend the truth and secure justice for the oppressed. It begins with the insistent claim that the militarizing of the Panth by the sixth Guru and the subsequent creation of the Khalsa by the tenth were strictly in accord with Nanak's own intention. For many the classic statement of this claim is to be found in the stirring words of Joseph Cunningham: "It was reserved for *Nanak* to perceive the true principles of reform, and to lay those broad foundations which enabled his successor *Gobind* to fire the minds of his countrymen with a new nationality, and to give practical effect to the doctrine that the lowest is equal with the highest in race as in creed, in political rights as in religious hopes."[7]

It was, in other words, Nanak's doctrine of equality which supplied the essential basis for later developments. Nanak had signaled the destruction of caste with his words of explicit denunciation. Gobind Singh sealed his intention by requiring all Khalsa entrants to drink the same water of initiation from a common cup. Nanak had proclaimed that deliverance from suffering and transmigration is available to all, regardless of how lowly or oppressed an individual might be. His successors, and notably Guru Gobind Singh, translated this doctrine into militant defence of the rights of all men. In the face of tyranny justice can be defended and maintained only by the use of force. If all other methods of redress have failed it is legitimate to draw the sword in the defense of righteousness. The obligation to perform this duty if need should arise must be accepted by every loyal follower of the Guru.[8]

Many see this summons to a new order and discipline as a sudden change, one which the tenth Guru dramatically thrust upon a startled Panth when he announced the inauguration of the Khalsa on the Baisakhi Day of 1699. The execution of his father by order of the Emperor Aurangzeb had convinced the youthful Guru that his followers must learn to defend justice with the sword, and that they must adopt an outward identity of a kind which would make craven concealment impossible. The actions of the sixth Guru, Hargobind, are recognized as a significant foreshadowing of the change which was to come, but the actual transformation belongs to the time of Guru Gobind Singh and specifically to the founding of the Khalsa in 1699.

This was the dominant view of the Singh Sabha period and it has been restated by Khushwant Singh in his widely read *A History of the Sikhs*.[9] More recently Jagjit Singh has developed this interpretation into a detailed theory of revolution, one which maintains that the period of the Gurus must be viewed as a whole and the Panth which they led as the progressive development of a single sustained ideal. "The Sikh movement was an organic growth of the Sikh religion or the Sikh view of life. The founding of the Sikh *Panth* outside the caste society in order to use it as the base for combatting the hierarchical set-up of the caste order, and the creation of the Khalsa for capturing the state in the interests of the poor and the suppressed, were only a projection, on the military and political plane, of the egalitarian approach of the Sikh religious thesis."[10]

The essence and common feature of these related interpretations is that they all attribute the historical development of the Sikh Panth (at least during the first three centuries of its existence) to the explicit intention of the Gurus. They thus represent a strictly ideological view. The Gurus envisaged a particular pattern for the Panth which they created, and the actual form which it assumed corresponded to their intention. It accordingly developed as a militant order with a particular range of external symbols because that is what the fundamental intention required. Guru Gobind Singh may have been responsible for engendering the spirit and proclaiming the actual form which the Khalsa was to assume, but he did so only because a basic egalitarian principle had already been enunciated by Guru Nanak. The intervening Gurus likewise contributed to the same process, each advancing the same basic ideal and formulating practical responses as circumstances demanded.

This interpretation has been contested on the grounds that it stresses intention and ideology much too strongly. There has been no suggestion that the Gurus lacked clear objectives, nor that they were ineffectual in the pursuit of their declared purposes. The point which this fourth interpretation seeks to make is that the weight of emphasis is elsewhere thrown much too strongly on preconceived intention as an explanation for subsequent developments; and that insufficient allowance is made for environmental factors. These factors include the social constitutency of the developing Panth, the economic context within which it evolved, and the influence of contemporary events such as those produced by local political rivalries and foreign invasion.

The claim embodied in this fourth interpretation was advanced in *The Evolution of the Sikh Community*, first published in 1975 but building on insights supplied by earlier writers.[11] This book (pp. 4–5) claimed as one of its purposes "to seek a more radical concept of development, one which will express a much more intricate synthesis of a much wider range of historical and sociological phenomena." The traditional explanation is, it suggested, much too simple and its use of sources much too narrowly selective. It should perhaps be added that the interpretation partly derives from a suspicion of many wide-ranging explanations based on the preconceived intentions of individuals, however influential those individuals may be. Within a narrow and immediate range such explanations can be wholly plausible, but not for a movement as complex and long-lived as the Sikh Panth.

The fourth interpretation thus claims that the progressive development of the Panth must be explained not merely in terms of purposeful intention but also (and in significant measure) by the influence of the social, economic and historical environment. This specifically includes such major features as the militant texture of the later Panth and the growth of the Rahit (the distinctive code of conduct associated with membership of the Khalsa).[12] As such it necessarily applies to the modern Panth as much as to the earlier, seeking to explain continuing controversies as well as agreed orthodoxy.

To those nurtured on Western historiography this fourth interpretation may well sound like an elementary statement of the received wisdom which, in general terms, all academic historians accept. If so it may simply reflect our own subjection to a particular tradition. The interpretation offered by *The Evolution of the Sikh Community* has been strongly attacked from within the Panth, with criticism focusing on two major features of the general theory. The first is its treatment of caste within the Panth. The second is its suggestion that the growth of militancy should be related to the traditions of a particular group within the Panth, namely those of the Jat caste.[13] Some attention has also been paid to its theory that the doctrine of the Guru's mystical presence within both Panth and Granth (community and sacred scripture) should be regarded as a belief developed over time rather than as the result of a pronouncement by Guru Gobind Singh.[14] Its claim (pp. 50–53) that the Rahit should likewise be viewed as a product evolved (and still evolving) over time seems so far to have escaped serious attack.

Because the views expressed in *The Evolution of the Sikh Community* are my own, and because I continue to hold those views, the brief summary of Sikh history which now follows will inevitably be informed by the fourth interpretation noted above. This means that the summary will incorporate a particular bias. No apology is offered for this feature, nor is there any suggestion that I regard the bias as misplaced. It is, however, important to remember that it will represent a minority view at certain crucial points. For the dominant traditional view one must look elsewhere.

Before he died in 1539 Guru Nanak appointed as his successor a disciple called Lahina, having bestowed on him the new name of Angad. Guru Angad was followed by Guru Amar Das, and he in turn by his son-in-law Guru Ram Das.[15] Thereafter the succession was confined to the male line of the Sodhi family descending from Guru Ram Das. His youngest son Arjan became the fifth Guru in 1581, and was followed in turn by his own son Hargobind in 1606. The succession was sometimes disputed, notably by Arjan's elder brother Prithi Chand, but an acknowledged 'succession was sustained and it seems that none of the rival contenders was able to detach a significant segment of the growing Panth.

Guru Arjan carries us into the seventeenth century and into a period of significant change for the Panth. Throughout the sixteenth century the Panth had continued to grow in numbers and to develop in terms of organization and definition. The early Gurus were obviously faithful to the original message of Nanak, repeating in endless variety his doctrine of release from the transmigratory cycle through the practice of *nām simaran* or meditation on the divine Name. As the numerical strength of the Panth increased administrative features which had been unnecessary during the time of the first Guru inevitably became a part of its regular life. It is still very difficult to determine in detail exactly what was happening during this sixteenth-century period, but the outlines seem clear and they confirm the reasonable expectation that the Nanak-panth was developing patterns and procedures, customs and rituals. It was (to use Cantwell Smith's term) crystallizing.

To some extent the principal features of this phase might be regarded as an implicit denial of a fundamental feature of Guru Nanak's own teachings. Nanak had laid the characteristic Sant emphasis on the futility of such external observances as temple-worship and pilgrimage, and of blind trust in the efficacy of sacred scriptures. The third Guru, Amar Das, evidently made his own village of Goindval a destination for pilgrims and it appears that he also gathered the materials which were to form the nucleus of the Adi Granth. Guru Ram Das excavated the pool known as Amritsar, and this and other sites became places of pilgrimage for devout members of the Panth. To perform *kīrtan* (the congregational singing of hymns) Sikhs assembled in dharam-salas and these buildings began to acquire the ritual connotations which we associate with the gurdwara (the successor of the dharam-sala).

There is nothing surprising about such developments. A growing and maturing community is bound to acquire shape and definition, replicating in institutional form many of the ideals which constituted the original message. The role of the Guru, the liberating influence of the sacred *bāṇī* (the utterances of the Gurus), and the spiritual equality of all believers were fundamental features of that original message as received by the early Sikhs. This being the case we can scarcely be surprised if the process of crystallization should produce appropriate customs and institutions.[16] With them came a rudimentary organization designed to maintain spiritual oversight of an expanding community and to receive the gifts offered to the Guru as devout expressions of allegiance. Guru Amar Das apparently organized the *mañjī* system which placed the more distant *saṅgats* (congregations) under his deputies, and each individual appointed to a manji came to be known as a *masand*. It was the duty of the masands to act as the Guru's vicars, guiding his growing flock and collecting their offerings.

The period of the fifth Guru, Arjan, is important for two main reasons. The first is that it was Guru Arjan who arranged for the Adi Granth to be recorded, conferring on the Panth a sacred scripture which was to acquire great symbolic power. The second is that Mughal interest and apprehension became evident during his time. The precise cause and circumstances of the fifth Guru's death may still be obscure, but it occurred while he was in Mughal custody and it made him the first Sikh martyr.

Babur, the first in the Mughal line, had descended from Afghanistan into India during the life-time of Guru Nanak and during the next half-century the dynasty had established rule over most of northern India.

At first the Sikhs attracted little Mughal attention, but as their numbers grew they began to be noticed. According to the traditional Sikh view it was Mughal hostility and the need to protect the victims of Mughal oppression which produced the first significant move towards the militarizing of the Panth. Guru Arjan is said to have advised his son Hargobind to carry arms, and it is believed that following his accession in 1606 Hargobind wore not one but two swords. The action was symbolic. Whereas one sword represented the Guru's continuing spiritual authority (*pīrī*) the other proclaimed a newly-assumed temporal role (*mīrī*). The three battles fought against Mughal forces during the time of Guru Hargobind may have been mere skirmishes, but an important decision had nevertheless been made and a major development initiated. The Panth was thereafter to be armed.

The alternative explanation does not deny the Guru's decision to take up arms, a tradition which is supported by strong evidence.[17] What it does propose is that Mughal hostility need not have been the only reason for the shift in policy. There were certainly Jats amongst the Guru's following and the rural location of the Panth's principal centers suggest that the Jats' numerical predominance of later centuries was probably developing by the time of the fifth and sixth Gurus.[18] The Jats are a people accustomed to bearing arms and to using them as a means of resolving disputes. If we are right in assuming that significant numbers were entering the Panth it obviously follows that a significant portion of the Panth's constituency bore arms as a matter of course.

This need not mean that they had previously worn arms when appearing before the Guru and it certainly does not mean that there had been a Jat take-over of any kind. What it does mean is that the bearing of arms was already an established custom for many Sikhs. It was, moreover, a custom which would be unlikely to generate strong disapproval on the part of the dominant Khatri leadership, apart from those with a strong commitment to the traditional role of the religious teacher. Khatris (as their name and some distinguished examples indicate) are by no means divorced from the use of arms. If this theory is correct it would mean that Guru Hargobind's change of policy was undertaken in the context of an existing tradition of arms-bearing, a tradition which largely derived from the attitudes and customs of a major component of the Panth's membership.

The same kind of problem recurs when we reach the end of the seventeenth century. A period of peace followed the skirmishes of the sixth

Guru's time and under the seventh Guru, Hari Rai (1644–61), the Panth attracted little attention from anxious Mughal authorities. The accession of a minor created internal problems during the brief period of the child Guru Hari Krishan (1661–64), but these were largely solved when he was followed by Guru Tegh Bahadur (1664–75). During the later years of Guru Tegh Bahadur, however, the Panth again attracted hostile Mughal attention, culminating with his execution by order of the Emperor Aurangzeb.

The beheading of Guru Tegh Bahadur in 1675 is a key point in Sikh historiography. Although there are two different traditions concerning the tenth Guru's decision to inaugurate the Khalsa order with its mandatory Rahit, the two are not dissimilar and both relate to the crisis caused by his father's execution. One tradition emphasizes the Guru's belief that sparrows had to be turned into hawks, that a new baptism and discipline should be introduced in order to convert his followers into men of steel.[19] The alternative tradition focuses on the Guru's conviction that his Sikhs, having shrunk from recognition at Tegh Bahadur's execution, should never again be permitted to conceal their identity.[20] The two traditions supplement each other and together they supply the standard explanation for the founding of the Khalsa. The actual event took place in 1699. Having dramatically introduced his new rite of sword-baptism (*khaṇḍe dī pāhul*) the Guru promulgated the Rahit which all who accept initiation must promise to observe.[21]

According to the traditional view this single event sealed and confirmed both the militant character of the Panth and the substance of the code which its members were thereafter to follow. Only one major addition was still to be made and this too resulted from an explicit command issued by the tenth Guru. Shortly before he died in 1708 Guru Gobind Singh decreed that at his death the line of personal Gurus should terminate. The Guru would thereafter be mystically present within the sacred scripture and the corporate community. The Guru Granth and Guru Panth would thus exercise the divine authority of the Guru, and all issues concerning belief or practice should be referred to them for guidance and (when necessary) for a formal decision.

The tradition is consistent, but doubts must persist. Questions must persist because the historical context of the Khalsa's foundation and subsequent development is considerably more complex than the simple tradition allows. There is, for example, the problem of the masands. The masands, as we have already noted, were the Gurus' representatives, responsible for shepherding scattered sangats (groups of disciples or congregations) and for collecting their offerings. Many of the masands had apparently become arrogant and corrupt, prompting the tenth Guru to suppress them. A portion of the Panth was evidently under the Guru's own direct supervision and this portion constituted his khalsa (*khālsā* being the word used for that part of a domain which is under the direct control of its central authority).[22] In commanding all loyal Sikhs to abandon the masands he was summoning them to join a khalsa which already existed.

This clear intention weakens the traditional stress on the militant purpose of the Khalsa inauguration, but it certainly does not destroy it. The true nature of the formalized Khalsa depends upon the Rahit and if Guru Gobind Singh did indeed promulgate the Rahit the traditional interpretation may still command general acceptance. It is here that real complexity is encountered and at this stage no one can predict the results that research will eventually produce. That the Guru did promulgate a system of belief and behavior no one need doubt. The problem concerns the nature of the new code which he personally enunciated, as opposed to those portions of the developed Rahit which evolved during the period following his death.

A detailed discussion of the Rahit will be offered in chapter 5. Here it can merely be noted that the evidence convincingly points to a period of major development during the course of the eighteenth century. Even the institution of the "Five Ks," that most famous feature of the Rahit, cannot be immune from this scrutiny. The Five Ks (*pañj kakke* or *pañj kakār*) are the five items, each beginning with the letter "k," which every initiated member of the Khalsa must wear. Most prominent of the five is the *kes* or uncut hair. The other four are the comb which is worn in the topknot of the uncut hair (*kaṅghā*), the steel bangle (*karā*), the sword or dagger (*kirpān*), and the distinctive shorts (*kachh*). In the oldest manuscript of the earliest extant rahit-nama (a recorded version of the Rahit) there is no reference to the Five Ks as such, although there is abundant emphasis on the uncut hair and the sword.[23] A later version of the same rahit-nama introduces five items which loyal Sikhs must embrace and three of these (*kachh, kirpān* and *kes*) figure in the Five Ks. The other two, however, are *bāṇī* (the sacred words of the scripture) and *sādh saṅgat* (the congregation of the faithful).[24]

This and other rahit-nama evidence seems plainly to point to a period of development during the course of the eighteenth century, a development which reflects pressures operating within the Panth or applied to it by external events. Two such pressures should be briefly noted. One is the presence of a substantial and highly active Jat constituency within the Panth. The other is the experience of protracted warfare through much of the century. Although it may be difficult to trace the actual emergence of specific details there can be no doubt that the Rahit was (and remains) an evolving tradition, and that some of its key features derive from the eighteenth-century experience of the Panth.

With regard to other aspects of the Panth's eighteenth-century experience the traditional and the evolutionary interpretations reconverge. This is the heroic period of Sikh history and from it emerge traditions of bravery and endurance which still fire the modern Panth. During the early decades of the century the Sikhs suffered vigorous hostility from their Mughal enemies, surviving to take advantage of the confusion which resulted from a series of Persian and Afghan invasions during the middle decades. Thereafter their strength continued to grow, divided at first but eventually united under the rule and expanding empire of Maharaja Ranjit Singh (1799–1839).

Rapid collapse followed the death of Ranjit Singh and by 1849 the Punjab had been annexed by the advancing British. The Panth seemed to be rapidly decaying and British observers confidently predicted its imminent demise. Their mistake leads us to the last of the great controversies which we shall note in this chapter. During the later years of the nineteenth century and the first three decades of the twentieth there occurred a notable revival, one which has left traditions powerfully present within the modern Panth. The credit for this revival is usually bestowed on the enlightened devotion of the leaders responsible for the Singh Sabha movement. The first Singh Sabha was founded in 1873 and although the movement as a whole was troubled by internal conflicts its active participants succeeded in promoting a reformed Sikhism of a highly durable quality.[25] Eventually it was overtaken by the more strident approach of the Akali movement which during the early 1920s conducted a non-violent campaign aimed at restoring the principal gurdwaras to orthodox Khalsa control.[26]

Having thus sketched the received version of the Singh Sabha and Akali movements we must note that here too questioning voices have been raised and that much remains to be done before anything resembling a consensus emerges. Reference was made earlier in this chapter to the most direct of the relevant criticisms, namely the claim that the

Singh Sabha version of the Khalsa identity should be regarded as a British creation. This creation, it is maintained, was subsequently adopted and embellished by a class elite within Sikh society. The general theory may be summarily rejected, but some of the questions which it raises should certainly be examined before they are put aside. In addition to British intentions and class interests these questions concern the issue of multiple identities within the nineteenth-century Panth and the influence of political circumstances on particular groups within it. The time for firm conclusions is still far off. The debate has scarcely begun.

This may seem an unsatisfactory note on which to end this survey, but it is an accurate impression of the current state of academic play. Few would suggest that a mass upheaval awaits us, that the old landmarks will be swept away leaving an entirely new landscape. The outline of Sikh history will retain its familiar features and the same figures will continue to dominate it. It is, however, likely that new interpretations will produce some considerable shifts in the understanding of that history. From the debate now under way there may yet emerge some very significant changes.

4

Sikh Doctrine

THIS chapter offers two elementary hypotheses, two simple notions which some might like to regard as axioms. The first may be enunciated as follows. A religious tradition can be understood only in its own terms rather than exclusively in translation. This, in practice, requires an understanding of the terminology which expresses the fundamentals of the tradition, an understanding which can seldom be achieved by means of single-word English translations. The second axiom follows from the first and to some extent merely restates it. It is that the essential outline of a religious tradition can be sketched by defining a series of key terms in an appropriate sequence.

If therefore we seek an understanding of the Sikh tradition we must concentrate our primary attention upon a carefully selected choice of terminology arranged in a logical order. Needless to say the selection which is offered here must be inadequate. It would plainly be impossible to present within such a limited space either a detailed analysis of individual doctrines or the closely integrated sequence which an ideal theology of Gurmat should eventually deliver. It should be possible, however, to indicate the elements of a system, hoping that someone within the Panth will one day correct it and spell it out in detail.

The paramount need for working from the tradition's own concepts and terminology can be illustrated by a brief examination of that most obvious of examples. We have all heard reasons why the word "God" is inappropriate as a translation when we move beyond the Christian tradition and some readers will find those reasons very cogent indeed. The Sikh example must surely offer strong support for the claim. The term which is traditionally used to express Guru Nanak's concept is *Akāl Purakh*, literally "the Timeless Being." Akal Purakh is a very different concept from the range of meaning covered by the English word "God" and if we persist in using the latter term we shall find it very difficult indeed to avoid its distinctive connotations. *Kartār* is another of Guru Nanak's terms for the Supreme Being in which the translation "Creator" communicates a range of meaning different from the Western sense. Some, it is true, claim the ability to be able to make the necessary adjustments and thus to invest the old word with new meaning. It is a claim which deserves to be met with considerable skepticism.[1]

This particular issue is a complicated one as far as the Sikh tradition is concerned. Complications arise partly because Nanak's own meaning is necessarily elusive and partly because the *Akāl Purakh* usage is accompanied by the more recent compound *Vāhigurū*. This, however, is the kind of problem which belongs to a later stage in the analysis. Any survey of the tradition must start with Guru Nanak and the word *Vāhigurū* has no place in his teachings. Today *Vāhigurū* is a more common term than *Akāl Purakh*, but in Nanak's time it was unknown and when it first came into use it meant "Praise to the Guru."[2]

Nanak actually employed many different words in giving expression to the ultimate reality which Sikh tradition calls *Akāl Purakh*. Some of these terms are traditional names such as Hari and Ram. Many more are words which designate his attributes, commonly as negatives which attempt in the traditional style to define reality in terms of what it is not. Indeed the word *a-kāl* or "timeless" is a conspicuous example. Nanak's meaning is necessarily elusive because his belief and practice were essentially mystical and in the last resort only those who comprehend Akal Purakh in their own mystical experience can truly grasp the meaning which human words endeavor to communicate. The final and all-embracing term is *alakh*. Akal Purakh is ineffable.

This does not mean, however, that Akal Purakh is altogether unknowable. On the contrary, the essential being of Akal Purakh is revealed for all to see if they will but open their eyes. We are brought to the word which can be regarded as the most important of all the many terms used by Nanak in order to communicate his understanding of Akal Purakh and of the way to liberation. And it should be noted in passing that a particular English word has just been used instead of another more common usage. The word was "liberation" and not "salvation," a choice based on the conviction that the latter term is altogether inappropriate in the Sikh context.

That important word in *nām*, frequently linked with *sati* to give the compound form *satinām*. The literal translation of *nām* is, of course, "name" and for once there is an English rendering which corresponds closely to the original. The problem is knowing what *nām* or "the Name" means in Nanak's repeated usage. A brief definition offered twenty years ago was "the total expression of all that God is."[3] Substitute Akal Purakh for God and you have a reasonable summary. The definition adds that the same reality can also be called the Truth, thus indicating the sense of the *satinām* compound.

The *nām* is everywhere around us and within us, yet man is rendered congenitally blind by *haumai*. This is another compound, one which comprises two forms of the first person singular pronoun. As such it signifies the powerful impulse to succumb to personal gratification, thus earning the kind of *karam* (karma) which holds a person firmly within the cycle of *sansār*. Birth follows death and suffering infuses all. Akal Purakh, however, looks graciously upon the suffering of mankind and through the *gurū* utters the *śabad* which communicates a sufficient understanding of the *nām* to those who are able to "hear" it. The Guru is thus the "voice" of Akal Purakh, mystically uttered within the *man* (heart–mind–spirit) of the devotee. The *śabad* or "Word" is the actual "utterance" and in "hearing" it a person awakens to the reality of the divine Name, immanent in all that lies around and within him.

The nature of the divine Name is itself determined by the *hukam* of Akal Purakh. This designates the divine order of the entire universe, an order which is synonymous with harmony. Liberation is achieved by means of bringing oneself within this harmony. An objective which is progressively attained by the strictly interior discipline of *nām simaran* or "remembering the *nām*." This discipline ranges from the simple repetition of an appropriate word or mantra (*nām japan*) through the devout singing of hymns (*kīrtan*) to sophisticated meditation. All are designed to bring the individual into accord with the *nām*, thus earning for him or her the kind of *karam* which provides release. The ultimate condition of blissful *sahaj* is achieved when the spirit ascends to *sach khaṇḍ* (the "realm of truth"), a goal which may be reached before the physical death which is its final seal.

As the one responsible for communicating this truth Nanak became the embodiment of the eternal *gurū* and those who succeeded him in the lineage which he established assumed the same role. Although the line included ten individuals there remained but one *gurū*, passing successively from one to the next as a single flame ignites a series of torches. Their compositions are known as *bāṇī* or *gurbāṇī* and the sum total of their teachings is of course Gurmat. The fifth in the succession, Guru Arjan, had the *bāṇī* of the first five Gurus recorded in a book (*granth*) in 1603–4, adding to it approved works by earlier representatives of the Sant tradition such as Namdev and Kabir. Upon the book was conferred the respect due to its authors and it was accordingly known as the Granth Sahib. Later, as the system of doctrine developed, it was to receive a further dignity.

The establishment of a spiritual lineage followed the first forming of a group of disciples. These were the original *sikh*, "learners" or Sikhs. As a group of devotees with a common loyalty and tradition they constituted a *panth* ("path" or "way") and because the first loyalty had been to Nanak they were known as the *Nānak-panth*. *Panth* is another of the key terms which refuses to yield a simple translation. This, however, is an analysis which is better postponed until the discussion of *khālsā*, for the two terms overlap to a considerable extent. It should be noted at this point because there will be reference to the following which the Gurus attracted and for this group of disciples the appropriate term is either *Nānak-panth* or simply *Panth*.

Before discussing *khālsā* there is an intermediate term to be introduced. During the period of Guru Arjan (1581–1606) the Nanak-panth became the object of Mughal suspicion and the Guru himself died in Mughal custody. According to tradition he responded to the developing threat of Mughal hostility by instructing his son, the future Guru Hargobind (1606–44), "to sit fully armed on his throne."[4] In obedience to this command Hargobind, having succeeded his father, symbolically donned two swords. One sword designated a newly-assumed temporal role (*mīrī*) while the other represented the spiritual authority which he had inherited from his five successors (*pīrī*).

The doctrine of *mīrī-pīrī* signals the Panth's immensely important shift towards militancy. This did not mean that the spiritual concerns of the earlier Nanak-panth had been renounced. On the contrary, these were explicitly affirmed throughout the remainder of the Gurus' period and the same emphasis continues to the present day. The change should not be understood, however, as the mere defending by military means of an unchanging theory of spirituality. It was a change which significantly affected the subsequent understanding and promulgation of Sikh doctrine. It is during the time of the tenth Guru, Gobind Singh, that the change emerges to full view. Akal Purakh is characteristically called *Sarab Loh*, "All-Steel," and the sword assumes a central significance in the doctrine and ritual of the Panth.

Thee I invoke, All-conquering Sword, Destroyer of Evil,
  Ornament of the brave.
Powerful your arm and radiant your glory, your splendour as
  dazzling as the brightness of the sun.
Joy of the devout and scourge of the wicked, Vanquisher of sin,
  I seek your protection.
Hail to the world's Creator and Sustainer,
  my invincible Protector the Sword.[5]

It is Akal Purakh who is here addressed, divinity made manifest in the burnished steel of the unsheathed sword. The intervening history of the Panth explains the change and appropriate terminology reflects it.

The sword thus introduced into Sikh doctrine and tradition figures prominently in *amrit sanskār*, the initiation ceremony marking entry into the recreated Panth of Guru Gobind Singh. The recreated Panth is, of course, the Khalsa. Although the term is correctly traced to the word *khālis* the immediate etymology seems not to be the common adjectival meaning of "pure." The Persian *khālis* had produced the form *khālsā*, used as a noun to designate lands under the direct administration of the crown or central authority. As the early Panth grew and expanded the supervision of an individual *saṅgat* (congregation) or small clusters of sangats was entrusted by the Gurus to vicars called *masands*. Some sangats, however, remained under the continuing supervision of the Guru as his *khālsā*. By the time of Guru Gobind many of the masands had become arrogant or corrupt and in commanding all Sikhs to abandon the masands the Guru simultaneously summoned them to join his *khālsā*.

All who heeded the Guru's summons and accepted invitation were required to observe the *rahit*, another key term. The Rahit comprises the outward symbols, the very specific rules of conduct, and the distinctive rituals which a Sikh of the Khalsa is expected to observe. As such it is a very important word indeed, one which should certainly be much better known. In its developed form it includes such celebrated features as the *pañj kakke* or "Five Ks" (the five items, each beginning with the letter "k" which a Khalsa Sikh should wear) and a rigorous ban on smoking.

We return now to the word "Panth." Are "Panth" and "Khalsa" synonyms? For some Khalsa Sikhs the answer is a firm "yes." Others, however, are obviously unwilling to adopt such a hard line, for in so doing they necessarily imply that many who call themselves Sikhs have no right to do so. The more obvious of these deregistered claimants are the so-called *sahaj-dhārī* Sikhs, men and women who affirm allegiance to the teachings of Nanak and his successors (particularly to the doctrine and practice of *nām simaraṇ*) but who decline to accept Khalsa initiation or the full rigors of the Rahit. Less obvious because they so closely resemble the Khalsa model are those who observe the outward forms required by the Rahit (particularly the *kes* or uncut hair) but who nevertheless fail to "take *amrit*" (i.e. undergo initiation). Such people are certainly not members of the Khalsa. Are they thereby disqualified from membership of the Panth also?

As we shall see, the ambiguity of this situation reflects a real ambivalence. With regard to the definition of the Khalsa there is no ambiguity, nor is there likely to be a problem in the minds of most of the uninitiated. For the latter the simple answer is that the Panth is a larger entity which contains Sikhs of the Khalsa together with many who for various reasons do not accept the full Khalsa discipline. The Khalsa may be regarded an an elite or as the "orthodox" version of the Sikh identity, but the Rahit need not be regarded as a code which automatically excludes all who do not meet its strict requirements. But what is the loyal Khalsa Sikh to think? If Guru Gobind Singh envisaged a purpose for the Khalsa surely that intention must apply to all who claim to be his disciples. Calling oneself a follower of Guru Nanak is certainly unacceptable if it implies a rejection of later developments within the Panth. The Guru is one and instructions issued by the tenth Guru are as binding on Sikhs as guidance given by the first.

The problem is a real one and at times of crisis (such as the recent past and immediate present) it can become serious. It is further complicated by the widespread existence of multiple identities in Punjabi society, with individuals moving freely from one to another or (more commonly) maintaining dual identities without any sense of incongruity. The question is one which the outsider is unable to answer except in strictly pragmatic terms. We may observe that many people claim to be Sikhs without taking *amrit* and that a substantial proportion of these people actually observe the more obvious requirements of the Rahit. Though their precise status may be a matter for concern outsiders are certainly not entitled to offer answers. The debate continues, advancing and receding as circumstances dictate. It has sometimes involved the terms *sikhī* and *singhī*, with the former used to describe the larger identity and the latter to designate the specific identity of the Khalsa.

The demarcation issue is not the only problem associated with this richly complex word "Panth." Another difficulty is signaled by attempts to supply single-word English translations, attempts which should serve to reinforce the point with regard to the translating of basic terminology. It is easy to dispense with one such suggestion, namely the word "church"; this still appears from time to time, but it is so patently inappropriate that it quickly creates uneasiness and is soon abandoned. Two other attempts have achieved a wider popularity and deserve a little more attention. One is "sect" and the other is "nation."

"Sect" is a word which has been dealt with already. It has had a long history, having acquired a firm hold on an early generation of European observers. Nowadays, however, the usage is inappropriate, for it implies the existence of an orthodoxy from which it deviates. For most users of this particular "translation" the orthodoxy from which Sikhism diverged was presumably "Hinduism." The latter term is itself unacceptable (particularly as a word designating an agreed orthodoxy) and even if it were viable the suggestion that the modern Sikh Panth can be described as its "sect" would be absurd. Such a usage is also regarded as highly offensive by many Sikhs. The word has run its misguided course and mercifully it is seldom heard nowadays except as a feature of the language of polemic.

For some people, of course, the use of "sect" derives from a cursory interpretation of the nature of the Panth rather than from any acquaintance with the actual word. The same applies, in an even more complex way, to the second example. British authors who, during the first half of the nineteenth century, referred to the Sikhs as a "nation" are most unlikely to have had the word *panth* in mind. Their usage obviously reflected the existence of the very visible kingdom of Maharaja Ranjit

Singh. The description, having slumped with Sikh political fortunes in the later nineteenth century, has since revived and during recent years it has been ardently promoted by advocates of a larger political autonomy for the Sikhs. This modern usage, though specifically associated with the Panth, involves some crucial shades of meaning. Hovering in the background is the word *qaum*, an Arabic term which having entered Punjabi through Persian has long since been thoroughly naturalized. The Panth constitutes a "nation" because the Sikhs are a *qaum*.

But does *qaum* really deliver "nation" as an appropriate translation? The issue is an exceedingly controversial one and great tact is required in order to preempt an overwrought response. In its original sense *qaum* means "a people who stand together" and the substance of this meaning has carried over to Punjabi usage. Arguably the word can best be translated today as "ethnic identity." What it certainly involves is a conflict of attitudes which continues to ramify through Sikh society. In a very real sense we are dealing with a problem of translation which, having emerged in English usage, has now returned to create confusion in Punjabi. This is not to suggest that the fundamental problem derives from linguistic misunderstanding. What it does suggest is that the linguistic issue accurately reflects a basic problem concerning corporate Sikh identity and that the basic problem has been seriously aggravated by linguistic misunderstanding.

Other terms which have figured prominently in the recent crisis will bring us back to clarity and firm definition. The founding of the Khalsa order and the decades of warfare which followed immediately thereafter remolded the traditions of the Panth, creating a heroic ideal which endures to the present day. The ideal is commonly perceived to be the *sant-sipāhī*, he who combines the spirituality of the devout believer (*sant*) with the bravery and obedience of the true soldier (*sipāhī*). The supreme exemplar is Guru Gobind Singh and to this ideal the loyal Khalsa must aspire.

Sant is an interesting term in that it has been required to do service for a succession of meanings. Is is also interesting because it provides another example of a word which has been skewed by its standard English translation. The temptation to insert an "i" has proved irresistible and *sant* has typically emerged as "saint." This is a misleading translation, regardless of which meaning may be indicated by the actual Punjabi usage.

The word *sant* derives from *sat* and thus designates in its basic sense one who knows the truth or comprehends reality. As such it came to be applied to a particular devotional tradition, the one with which Guru Nanak himself was affiliated. The word passed into standard Sikh usage through the works of Nanak and his successors, bearing a strong sense of devotion and intimacy associated with the concept of the *sādh saṅgat* or *satsaṅg* (the congregation of true believers). Increasingly it came to designate an elite within the sangat and thus acquired the status of an actual title. Those who have followed recent events in the Punjab will appreciate how influential some Sants have now become. Such men are preceptors whose primary function is to give instruction in the beliefs and traditions of the Panth. These traditions stress worldly involvement as well as spiritual devotion and it should thus come as no surprise to discover that men bearing the title of Sant are to be found amongst the political leaders of the modern Panth.[6]

Such men teach the *mīrī-pīrī* tradition and those who personally match the ideal will be regarded as *sant-sipāhī*. Other terms used in current Sikh politics also recall the militant traditions of the Panth. The dominant political party is the Akali Dal or Akali Army. Each territorial unit of the party is designated a *jathā* (military detachment) and an organized political campaign is a *morchā* (facing the enemy). A particularly important and lengthy political struggle may be called a *dharam yudh*, "a war fought in defense of *dharam*."

This leads us to another of the words which defy translation, an instance which will have a familiar ring. *Dharam* is the Punjabi version of *dharma*, but one should not assume that the two are identical in terms of meaning and connotation. Although the Panth preserves the caste structure of society it is non-caste in theory and it thus rejects the strict definition of *dharma* as the obligations associated with a particular caste identity. In Sikh usage the stress moves away from the individual to the Panth or to society as a whole, and the sense connoted by *dharma* involves the moral order which alone provides a sure foundation for harmony and social stability. An attack on *dharam* is an attack on justice, on righteousness, and on the moral order generally. It must be defended at all costs and when other means have all failed the defenders of *dharam* must resort to the sword.

None of this should suggest that the Panth exists only to breathe fire or wield naked swords. The use of force is certainly sanctioned in a famous couplet attributed to Guru Gobind Singh[7] but is is authorized only in defence of *dharma* and only as a last resort. In times of disturbance or crisis one is liable to forget that the gurdwaras, though legitimately used for political purposes, are primarily places of worship. We have come to yet another of the key terms. The word *gurduārā* (anglicized as "gurdwara") can be translated as either "the Guru's door" or "by means of the Guru's [grace]."[8] Since earliest days members of the Panth have gathered together in satsangs to sing kirtan (sacred songs, specifically those composed by the Gurus and eventually those which are recorded in the Granth Sahib). The building in which a devotional gathering was held was originally known as a *dharam-sālā*, but during the course of the eighteenth century this term was progressively supplanted by *gurduārā*.

The change presumably occurred because of the increasingly common presence within these buildings of the Guru himself in the form of the sacred scripture. Following the death of Guru Gobind Singh the mystical *guru* remained present within the scripture which Guru Arjan had compiled a century earlier. The Granth Sahib thus became the Guru Granth Sahib, sharing this dignity with the gathered Panth which likewise incorporated the mystical presence of the eternal Guru. In practice the scripture has proved to be the effective vehicle and its mere presence constitutes any room or building a gurdwara.

Within a gurdwara most activity focuses on the sacred volume or its contents. The standard pattern of worship consists largely of the singing of kirtan, led by qualified members of the sangat or by professional hymn-singers called *rāgīs*. At appropriate times *karāh prasād* (sanctified food) is distributed to all who are present and *kathā* may be delivered. This consists of an exposition of the scriptures or perhaps the narrating of an incident from the lives of the Gurus or from later Sikh history. *Kathā* is normally the responsibility of the gurdwara's *granthī*.

We come to yet another of the terms which has been misunderstood during the course of the recent political crisis. A *granthī* is a person who serves as the custodian of a gurdwara, with responsibility for the maintenance of the shrine and the conduct of its routine rituals. Most are humble men serving small gurdwaras, but the few who are appointed to prominent shrines acquire a larger dignity. Most prominent of all is the Chief Granthi of Harimandir in Amritsar (known to foreigners as the Golden Temple).

In recent times the Chief Granthi of the Golden Temple has come to be regarded as one of seven "High Priests" of the Panth. Five of the others are the Jathedars (or "Commanders") of the five *takhats* or "thrones," gurdwaras with a unique role and dignity. Special decisions affecting the temporal welfare and politics of the Panth are taken before Akal Takhat, the building which faces the Golden Temple and which was so seriously damaged during the army assault in June 1984. Akal Takhat is thus the principle focus of the Panth's worldly concerns, supported by similar institutions in Anandpur, Damdama, Patna, and Nander. The takhats are highly revered as institutions, and their custodians are accorded a certain measure of dignity and respect. Each takhat is also served by granthis and the Chief Granthi of Akal Takhat has been recognized as one of the "High Priests."

It is, however, wholly incorrect to describe these two Granthis and five Jathedars as "High Priests." The Panth recognizes no priesthood and by no stretch of the popular imagination can these seven men be legitimately regarded as priests. Moreover, they are not particularly "high." All receive their appointments by committee decisions and each can be removed by the same process. It has been convenient in some circles to treat them as "high" during the recent crisis in order to lend weight to policy statements and claims which are routed through them. Five of the seven are appointed by the Sikh organization which controls the main gurdwaras in the Punjab (the Shiromani Gurdwara Parbandhak Committee) and the remaining two have been vulnerable to central government pressure because their seats in Patna and Nander are well beyond the borders of the Punjab. The media have picked up the term "High Priests" and in persistently using it have distorted our understanding of both the nature of the Panth and the mechanics of the recent crisis.

If one is seeking genuine authority in the Panth one should examine the term *pañj piāre*, "the Cherished Five." When inaugurating the Khalsa Guru Gobind Singh chose five Sikhs of proven loyalty to receive the first baptism and then to administer it to the Guru himself and to others. All initiation ceremonies have since been conducted by groups of *pañj piāre* and important decisions concerning a sangat may likewise be entrusted to them. This is not the end of questions of authority, however, for one may well have to investigate those who stand behind the *pañj piāre*. There can be no doubt that the issue of authority within the Panth is an exceedingly difficult one.

One last word which deserves to be mentioned is *sevā*, yet another example of a term which undergoes a shift in meaning when introduced in its standard English translation. The translation "service" can easily suggest the kind of welfare activity which is intended to assist a community or alleviate individual suffering. *Sevā* certainly embraces these purposes, at least within the modern understanding of the term, but its primary meaning designates service to a gurdwara. It is another of the words which, in the full richness of its meaning and connotation, defies easy translation.

As such it reinforces the claim that only through careful analysis of such terminology can the inner meaning of a culture or a tradition be penetrated. In addition, by inducting such words into English usage, it may be possible to diminish misunderstanding and distortion. The terminology may often seem intimidating, but the inducements are substantial; with diligence and perseverance there are considerable rewards.

5

Who Is a Sikh?

W HO is a Sikh? *Sikh Rahit Maryādā*, the standard manual of Sikh
doctrine and behavior, provides a succinct answer:

> A Sikh is any person who believes in God (Akal Purakh); in the ten
> Gurus (Guru Nanak to Guru Gobind Singh); in Sri Guru Granth
> Sahib, other writings of the ten Gurus, and their teachings; in the
> Khalsa initiation ceremony instituted by the tenth Guru; and who does
> not believe in any other system of religious doctrine. [1]

But is this statement really a sufficient answer to the question? Like
all such summaries of a religious tradition it inevitably glosses over complexity, skirting essential issues and reducing diversity to a single simple
model. The model which it offers is the normative Khalsa definition
and it should be acknowledged at the outset that there have always been
other definitions of Sikh identity. But it is a fact that the Khalsa definition has long since established its claim to be regarded as the ortho-

dox form of Sikhism. Although the continuing problem of non-Khalsa versions of Sikh identity is one which must be discussed later, in order to examine the nature of orthodox Sikhism it is necessary first to discuss the doctrine and practice of the Khalsa. The first answer to the question "Who is a Sikh?" should be that he or she is a Sikh of the Khalsa.

It was not always so. The inauguration of the Khalsa as a formal order and discipline took place 200 years after Guru Nanak first began to preach the doctrine of deliverance through the practice of *nām simaraṇ*. Although proponents of alternative Sikh identities commonly draw pointed attention to this feature it presents no problems as far as the Khalsa theologian is concerned. It is adequately covered by the fundamental Sikh doctrine of the Guru. The Guru, or mystical "voice" of Akal Purakh, is a single consistent authority, present within the Panth since first it was established. For more than two centuries it spoke through a succession of ten Masters (Guru Nanak to Guru Gobind Singh) and since the death of the tenth it has continued to speak through the sacred scripture (the Guru Granth) and the corporate community (the Guru Panth). The divine wisdom of the eternal Guru has been available to succeeding generations of Sikhs, guiding them as circumstances change into fresh decisions and new patterns. By the end of the seventeenth century circumstances had indeed changed, and it was to meet new challenges that Guru Gobind Singh took his momentous decision to reconstitute the Panth.

Traditional accounts describe the actual inauguration of the Khalsa in graphic detail. News was spread within the Panth that the annual festival to be celebrated on Baisakhi Day 1699 was to be a particularly significant event and that Sikhs should gather before the Guru on that occasion. After the expectant crowd had assembled all were stunned by the proclamation which the Guru issued. Five Sikhs were needed, he declared, five Sikhs who were prepared to offer their heads as a sacrifice. This summons was greeted with an understandable lack of enthusiasm, but eventually a loyal Sikh called Daya Singh offered himself and was led by his Master into a nearby tent. The thud of a falling sword was heard and when the Guru returned it was a blood-stained weapon which he carried. He repeated his demand and one by one four more Sikhs trooped into the place of slaughter, each to lose his head. The Guru then revealed what had actually happened inside the tent. Each of the five heroes had retained his head and in their place five goats had been slain. The five heroes were the original *Pañj Piāre*, the "Cherished Five" chosen for their bravery and total loyalty as the nucleus of a new order.[2]

Having thus chosen the foundation members of his new order and having initiated them with the new rite of sword-baptism (*khaṇḍe dī pāhul*) the Guru is said to have received the same baptism from their hands. He then delivered a sermon, explaining his reasons for introducing the new order and enunciating the code of conduct which its initiated members were to follow. He was, in other words, proclaiming the Rahit and it is the Rahit which defines in very specific terms the pattern of belief and practice which the Khalsa Sikh must observe. Tradition readily acknowledges that certain features of the Rahit were already a part of the pre-Khalsa pattern and it records that one major addition (the conferring of the Guru's authority on the Granth and the Panth) was made nine years later. It clearly implies, however, that the substance of the Rahit had been delivered to the Khalsa by the time the tenth Guru died. The Rahit remains thereafter the sole and sufficient statement of Khalsa doctrine, ritual and personal behavior. As such it supplies the standard definition of Sikh orthodoxy and Sikh identity.

Much that is contained in this popular version of the 1699 proceedings is open to serious question and although certain features receive support from near-contemporary sources others do not.[3] At this point the only feature which need concern us is the promulgating of the Rahit. One would expect that a statement so central to the life and purpose of the reconstituted Panth would have been committed to writing at an early stage and at least within the lifetime of Guru Gobind Singh. The Guru did indeed issue *hukam-nāmās* or "letters of command" to particular individuals and sangats, and the examples which survive incorporate items which would certainly have been included in any systematic statement of the complete Rahit. This, however, was a form of communication which had been used by some of his predecessors and although the surviving examples provide valuable illustrations of contemporary practice they cannot have been intended primarily as vehicles of the Rahit in any full or systematic form.[4]

No such systematic statement survives from the actual period of the Guru's lifetime. Randhir Singh has assumed that manuals or comprehensive statements would certainly have been prepared for use by the Guru's emissaries in order to instruct scattered sangats in their newly-established Khalsa faith.[5] These manuals, it is implied, must since have been lost. Others have drawn attention to the upheavals of the period immediately following 1699, suggesting that the urgency of conflict would leave little time for careful recording of what otherwise could be effectively communicated by word of mouth and visible example.

The fact that a distinctive code of conduct was operative by the early decades of the eighteenth century is indicated by references occurring in Sainapati's *Gur Sobhā* (Radiance of the Guru). *Gur Sobhā* is a narrative poem which, as its title suggests, belongs to the hagiographic gur-bilas genre.[6] It is a work of very great significance in terms of tracing the development of Sikh ideals, not least because it supplies an early selection of Rahit items. Unfortunately its potential significance is considerably diminished by the fact that its actual date has yet to be conclusively settled. The two contending dates are 1711 and 1745. If the earlier of the two could be definitively established the importance of *Gur Sobhā* would be greatly enhanced, for this would place the work very close to the death of Guru Gobind Singh in 1708.

Even with its precise date undetermined, however, *Gur Sobhā* remains a work of great significance. There can be little doubt that it belongs to the first half of the eighteenth century and in terms of the available sources for tracing Khalsa development this makes it very early indeed. Amongst the Rahit items which it offers are an insistence on the time-honored practice of *nām simaraṇ* and a categorical denunciation of hookah-smoking and cutting the hair.[7]

Gur Sobhā remains, however, a narrative poem. It makes no effort to enunciate the Rahit in systematic or comprehensive terms and accordingly it cannot strictly be regarded as a rahit-nama (a recorded version of the Rahit). Works which can legitimately be regarded as rahit-namas present an even wider range of problems. As we have just indicated, no rahit-nama survives from the actual lifetime of Guru Gobind Singh. There are, however, several such works claiming to record instructions which their writers received directly from the Guru before he died. These works form the rahit-nama corpus as it existed prior to the composing of the modern twentieth-century code. In no case can we accept a rahit-nama's claim that it reports injunctions received directly from the Guru and, as we shall see, the problems associated with dating them and placing them in their appropriate contexts are far from simple. There is, however, no doubt about their potential value as indicators of Khalsa development, nor of their importance as standards to which later generations have appealed in the ongoing effort to define normative Khalsa practice.

The rahit-namas which appear prior to the twentieth century can be divided according to form into three groups.[8] All offer statements, brief or lengthy, of what a Khalsa Sikh is expected to believe and how he or she should act. Four of the rahit-namas are brief works expressed in simple Punjabi verse. Three are lengthy prose collections, and the remaining two are brief works in prose. All nine claim or clearly imply derivation from the specific words of Guru Gobind Singh, posing as products of his actual intention rather than as responses to any subsequent period of Khalsa experience.

Of the four verse rahit-namas two are attributed to Bhai Nand Lal, the distinguished member of the tenth Guru's entourage whose Persian poetry commands great reverence within the Panth. These two are briefly entitled *Praśan-uttar* (Catechism) and *Tanakhāh-nāmā* (Manual of Penances). The former (plainly misnamed) is more discursive than the usual rahit-nama, concentrating on an exposition of the doctrine of the mystical Guru and stressing the believer's obligation to practice *nām simaraṇ*. By contrast the *Tanakhāh-nāmā* follows the typical format. Having listed various practices to be spurned or observed, it concludes with a stirring assurance of the future glory awaiting the Khalsa. Its final words continue to exercise an immense influence:

> *rāj karegā khālsā, āki rahahi na koi.*
> *khvār hoi sabh milainge, bachahi saran jo hoi.*

> The Khalsa shall rule, no enemy shall remain.
> All who endure suffering and privation shall be brought to
> the safety of the Guru's protection.[9]

The remaining verse rahit-namas, attributed respectively to Prahilad Singh (or Prahilad Rai) and Desa Singh, also follow the standard form. Like the two works bearing Nand Lal's name both claim to record firsthand information. Prahilad Singh is said to have been with Guru Gobind Singh in Abchalnagar (the town of Nanded in the Deccan) during the period immediately preceding the Guru's death there. According to the rahit-nama's brief prologue the Guru evidently realized that the Rahit should be recorded in order that the Khalsa might know its duty after he was no longer present in the flesh. He therefore summoned Prahilad Singh for this specific purpose and dictated the Rahit to him.[10] The rahit-nama attributed to Desa Singh similarly claims to record the Guru's words, supplemented by information received from Nand Lal.[11]

This same claim is made even more insistently by one of the three prose rahit-namas which offer detailed statements of the Rahit. Chaupa Singh Chhibbar was closely associated with Guru Gobind Singh, first as his khiḍāvā (adult playmate), then as his tutor, and finally as a trusted servant and counselor. Such a person might well claim intimate knowledge of the Guru's ideals and intentions. The Chaupā Siṅgh Rahit-nāmā does indeed make this claim, recording in profuse detail the many injunctions which the Guru is said to have issued for the benefit of the Khalsa.[12]

Within this lengthy work the Rahit material is gathered into two separate sections. One randomly lists actions which the Khalsa Sikh should perform or avoid; and the other specifies the many breaches of the Rahit for which an erring Khalsa should be required to do penance (tanakhāh).[13] The remainder of the work is devoted to various anecdotes from the life-story of Guru Gobind Singh, including a variant version of the founding of the Khalsa; to vigorous denunciations of the men who assumed leadership in the Khalsa following the Guru's death; and finally to promises of the apocalyptic glory which will accompany the arrival of Kalki and the consequent dawning of the long-awaited Satiyuga.[14]

The other two lengthy rahit-namas both belong to a much later period than the Chaupā Siṅgh Rahit-nāmā, though this does not mean any retreat from the standard claims to authenticity. In their present form both belong to the middle portion of the nineteenth century and at least one of them may well have originated at this time. This is the Prem Sumārag (or Param Sumārag), a work which begins with an announcement of imminent cosmic disaster and then details in an unusually systematic form the way of life which the Khalsa should follow.[15] The Sau Sākhī or "Hundred Episodes" is also vitally concerned with the troubles which must afflict the Panth and with prophecies of the rewards which await the faithful. In its extant form (and possibly in its origins) this particular work has been associated with the Namdhari sect and with the agitation which it conducted during the early period of British rule in the Punjab.[16]

This leaves the two prose rahit-namas which confine their attention to the Rahit and deal with it briefly. One of the two (a third work attributed to Nand Lal) is always found in association with the Chaupā

Siṅgh Rahit-nāmā. The few manuscripts which record the *Chaupā Siṅgh Rahit-nāmā* also append this short and fragmentary statement as a supplement.[17]

Finally there is the rahit-nama attributed to Daya Singh, first of the Panj Piare to offer his head at the founding of the Khalsa in 1699. Whereas the Nand Lal prose rahit-nama is certainly an eighteenth-century product the Daya Singh version seems plainly to date from the nineteenth century.[18] This feature is a further reminder that claims to represent the direct dictation of the Guru or a first-hand record of his pronouncements must always be regarded with profound skepticism. Indeed, one can go further and affirm that no extant rahit-nama sustains its claims in this regard. All are removed, to a greater or lesser extent, from the lifetime of Guru Gobind Singh.

That conclusion, needless to say, leaves the considerable problem of which rahit-namas qualify for the "lesser extent" status and which must be more distantly removed from the founder of the Khalsa. Later in this chapter I shall return to this problem, together with the associated difficulty of identifying actual contexts and the varying interests represented by each claimant.

Such issues were a part of the larger problem of authenticity which confronted the more ardent of the Singh Sabha reformers at the end of the nineteenth century. That Guru Gobind Singh had promulgated the Rahit was a tradition which could and must be accepted without question. But did the extant rahit-namas fully and faithfully record the Rahit as delivered by the Guru? Plainly, it seemed, they did not offer wholly reliable versions, for some of their injunctions seemed manifestly to be in conflict with enlightened belief. Although the Muslim rulers of the Guru's own time may have been cruel tyrants some of the items directed against Muslims (all Muslims and not just the perverse rulers) appeared rather too fierce for the educated leaders of the late nineteenth-century Panth. Other injunctions, it seemed, offered little more than superstition, and some were patently in conflict with the egalitarian ideals of the Khalsa. The *Chaupā Siṅgh Rahit-nāmā* was vulnerable on all three counts, producing such unacceptable examples as the following:

A Gursikh . . . should never become friendly with a Muslim, nor should he ever trust his sword. . . . Never trust the oath of a Muslim.

He who extinguishes a fire with water left over after drinking violates the Rahit.

He who administers baptism of the sword to a Sikh woman violates the Rahit.

Any Gursikh who is a Brahman should receive twice the service [and consideration that other Sikhs receive].[19]

The problem thus posed by the extant rahit-namas produced three different responses. One response was to prepare commentaries on the Rahit in general, or on those features of it which Sikhs of the Singh Sabha period perceived to be of particular importance. Some of their authors could be regarded as conservative upholders of received practice. These were the Sanatan Sikhs, a prominent example being Avatar Singh Vahiria who in 1894 published his *Khālsā dharam-śāstar* and in 1914 issued a substantial work of the same title which he had compiled.[20] Arrayed against them were the insistent reformers of the Tat Khalsa or "True Khalsa," radical men who increasingly sustained their right to speak as the authentic voice of the Panth. The general term "Singh Sabha" usually refers to these men, though one may not be aware of the fact.

The first Singh Sabha was founded in 1873 and as the Tat Khalsa gradually took shape its first endeavors concentrated on single issues, particularly those which might signal a distinctive Sikh identity as opposed to Hindu tradition and practice. Amongst the single issues the most conspicuous was the question of how Sikhs were to be married. Whereas earlier ritual had incorporated a sacred fire (thus implying obvious Hindu connotations) the Tat Khalsa reformers insisted on the Anand marriage ceremony as the only rite acceptable for Sikhs. This order involved circumambulation of the Guru Granth Sahib in place of the sacred fire, thus utilizing a major feature of the Rahit to assert a separate Sikh identity.[21] Other issues concentrated the debate on items which expressed a Khalsa identity as opposed to the generalized Sikh variant (the variant which accommodated the so-called *Sahaj-dhārī* or non-Khalsa Sikh).[22]

This was a truly radical approach, for the Tat Khalsa was signaling for the first time its basic difference from Hindu society. Alone, however, it was not enough. Debates and publications of this kind could obviously contribute to a rediscovery and redefinition of the Rahit, but they were insufficient. A systematic statement was also required, one which would carry the process beyond commentary and express the whole of the historic Rahit in a single authoritative document.

The second of the Tat Khalsa responses moved a step nearer to this objective. In 1898 Kahn Singh of Nabha published *Guramat Sudhākar* in Hindi, following it with a Punjabi edition in 1901.[23] *Guramat Sudhākar* was a compendium of works relating to the person and period of Guru Gobind Singh. Inevitably this included a selection from the rahit-namas and in editing the materials which were available to him Kahn Singh implicitly expressed a particular interpretation of them. Although his selections were presented as abridged versions of extant rahit-namas they are more accurately described as expurgated versions. What this implied was that the pure Rahit enunciated by the tenth Guru had subsequently been corrupted by ignorant or malicious transmitters of the tradition. By eliminating all that conflicted with reason and sound tradition (as understood by such men as Kahn Singh) one might hope to restore the pristine Rahit.

If in fact this was Kahn Singh's hope it was doomed to certain disappointment. Quite apart from the problem of distinguishing sound from spurious tradition there was the generally unsystematic form of the extant rahit-namas and the patchy nature of the material which they actually presented. No existing rahit-nama, purged or marginally supplemented, could satisfy the Singh Sabha reformers' insistence on a clear definition of Khalsa identity. Only a new statement would meet the need. A new rahit-nama had to be produced, one which would give clear and systematic expression to the Rahit as preserved in historical documents and sound tradition.

This recognition produced the third response to the problems posed by the extant rahit-namas, one which was eventually to prove definitive for twentieth-century purposes. A first attempt was made in the years 1910 to 1915. Concentrating on what were perceived to be appropriate Khalsa rituals it endeavored to produce acceptable rubrics and procedures for distinctively Khalsa ceremonies. The result of this attempt was issued in the latter year as *Guramat Prakāś Bhāg Sanskār*, a work which incorporated Rahit injunctions within suggested orders for various rituals.[24]

Following its first publication the manual achieved only a limited success and interest was soon deflected by the Akali agitation of 1920–25. This campaign produced the Shiromani Gurdwara Parbandhak Committee or SGPC (chosen by a general Sikh electorate to administer the principal gurdwaras)[25] and it was the SGPC which initiated the next effort to produce an agreed statement of the Rahit. In 1931 it resolved to commission a new rahit-nama. Although a sub-committee appointed for this purpose had produced a draft within a year a series of delays postponed final approval until 1945. The new rahit-nama was eventually published by the SGPC in 1950 under the title *Sikh Rahit Maryādā* (The Sikh Code of Conduct).[26]

Sikh Rahit Maryādā is not a model of clear organization nor of coherent presentation. In spite of its lengthy period of gestation it shows signs of haste and it leaves some important issues insufficiently defined. Its primary division of the Rahit into "Personal Discipline" and "Panthic Discipline" is difficult to defend, and the all-important question of fundamental authority remains unanswered. Ultimate authority is plainly declared to be the dual right of Granth and Panth, but radical ambiguity persists in that the translating of mystical authority into actual decisions remains only partially defined. Moreover, as we noted at the beginning of this chapter, it is a statement of Khalsa orthodoxy rather than a code for all who might regard themselves as Sikhs, clearly implying that there is an approved Khalsa style and that alternative Sikh identities are ipso facto unacceptable. This, it should be emphasized, is not explicitly declared to be the case. As with the problem of practical authority the nettle remains ungrasped.

In spite of these shortcomings *Sikh Rahit Maryādā* has so far stood the test of time remarkably well. It has run through numerous editions, it has admitted very little in the way of amendment,[27] and it has absolutely no rivals. The SGPC continues to issue it, both in its original Punjabi and in English translation; and if a Sikh seeks an answer to any problem of personal observance or Khalsa ritual *Sikh Rahit Maryādā* is the rahit-nama to which he or she is likely to turn. Here care must be taken not to exaggerate its importance. The answers to such questions will more commonly be sought orally from a Sikh with a reputation for learning or piety, or, in some circumstances, they may be ascertained by opening the Guru Granth Sahib at random and using it as an oracle. If, however, the appeal is to be made to a rahit-nama *Sikh Rahit Maryādā* will normally supply the means. In the pages of this brief manual will be found answers to many of the standard questions, and there can be no doubt that it has significantly contributed to the maintenance of a normative orthodoxy.

Does it then follow that *Sikh Rahit Maryādā* has succeeded in capturing the substance of the historical Rahit and that diligent reference to its pages will make it possible to produce a sufficient answer to the question of who is a Sikh? Some will insist that the answers to both of these questions should be affirmatives, and given its regular imprimatur it may be assumed that this remains the official view of the SGPC. Should we agree? It may be regarded as impertinent for an outsider to question these answers, and such a response would indeed by justified if the questioning were to suggest that the outsider is telling Sikhs what they should believe. There are nevertheless questions which should be raised before final conclusions are drawn. In the sincere hope that these questions will be regarded as neither impertinent nor irrelevant I will now put them. Some relate to the historic development of the Rahit and others to its contemporary application.

The first question concerns the origin and constancy of the Rahit. It is a question which is bound to invoke differing beliefs concerning the actual nature of the Rahit, and differing beliefs will produce different answers. Those who believe that the substance of the Rahit must be traced fully and directly to the intention of Guru Gobind Singh will offer one set of answers. At the other extreme those who perceive it as the mutating product of an evolving society will give a different set. Others, simultaneously attracted to both views, will endeavor to find a compromise which accommodates both the Guru's autonomous purpose and the influence of external pressures.

The question leads back to the conflict between traditional scholarship and rationalist historiography which we noted in the third chapter. Those who subscribe to the unyielding, uncompromising variety of traditional scholarship will insist that the essence of the Rahit, complete in all its fundamental features, was present in the intention of Guru Gobind Singh and that it must have been promulgated before his death in 1708. The actual sources make this view very difficult to sustain. The variant versions of the Rahit which appear in the earlier rahit-namas clearly indicate that much of the Rahit crystallized during the course of the eighteenth century and that a fully-developed version is not available until we move into the nineteenth century.

This is certainly not to suggest that none of the major elements was promulgated prior to the Guru's death, nor that the emergence of a recognizable Rahit was delayed until the end of the eighteenth century. What it does suggest is that a process which was already under way by

1708 continued to operate through succeeding decades, generating in response to eightcenth-century pressures several of the elements which feature prominently in the traditional Khalsa Rahit. These elements were subsequently purged, supplemented and restated during the period of the Singh Sabha reform movement, late in the nineteenth century and early in the twentieth. The reforming process eventually produced the Rahit as we know it today. Having thus evolved over a lengthy period it continues to develop, responding slowly to contemporary pressures and producing the new emphases which progressively remold it.

There are actually two separate issues involved in this general question of Rahit development, though the two are intimately related. One concerns origins and the other sequence: From where did the various items come, and when did they variously enter the Panth's conventions, thus becoming features of the orthodox Rahit? Linking the two is the question of cause: Why did particular items become features of Khalsa belief and practice?

Some items are easily explained, in terms either of origin or of timing and occasionally in terms of both. The strong rahit-nama insistence on the practice of *nām simaran* is an example of a feature which presents no problem at this level. The devotional discipline had been central to the teachings of the Panth ever since the time of Guru Nanak and it has retained its eminence through the period of rahit-nama growth. There are certainly problems to be encountered when one proceeds to ask just what was understood by such terms as *nām simaran* or *nām japan* at different times and by different people. This opens up a new range of issues which must be immediately put aside at least for now. For present purposes it is sufficient to note an unquestioning acceptance of some form of *nām simaran* as a primary feature of the Rahit at all stages of its development. It is a feature which illustrates one of the early roots of the Rahit and also its long-term continuity.

Other major items are less easy to identify in terms of origin, cause or sequence. The *pañj kakke* or Five Ks provide a conspicuous example, one to which I drew attention during the earlier discussion of tradition in chapter 3. The verdict of modern tradition is clear and wholly unambiguous. According to modern belief the Five Ks were introduced as a primary and essential feature of the Rahit at the inauguration of the Khalsa in 1699. As such they derive directly from the deliberate intention of Guru Gobind Singh, a purpose which is to be explained in terms of the Guru's determination that never again should his Sikhs be able to conceal themselves. This tradition is called into serious question by the testimony of eighteenth-century sources. With regard to the *kes* (the uncut hair) there is emphatic agreement that this feature is a mandatory requirement for all Sikhs of the Khalsa, and there is also repeated emphasis on the obligation to carry a sword.[28] The other three items, however, are much less certain and there seems to be no doubt that the actual concept of the five-k status belongs to a period well into the eighteenth century.[29]

This conclusion contributes something to our understanding of the sequence without telling us anything about the actual origins of the individual Ks or the reasons for their introduction into the Rahit. There is no cause to question the tradition that Guru Gobind Singh wanted his Sikhs to be visible and if (as seems likely) the *kes* was formally established within the Rahit during his lifetime the traditional answer may well be a correct one as far as this particular item is concerned. This, it must be emphasized, concerns the induction of the practice into the Rahit, not its actual origin. It still leaves open the strong possibility that its origin should be traced to the Jat custom of leaving the hair uncut, a possibility which may also explain some of the other Ks. By now it must surely be evident that any adequate analysis of the historical Rahit is bound to be an exceedingly complex task, and that there is still a long way to go in terms of explaining it.

Another interesting example is provided by the strict ban on smoking. This, as *Gur Śobhā* makes clear, is an early entrant into the Rahit,[30] but from where did it come and why is it thus emphasized as an essential mark of the loyal Sikh? Although it is unlikely that concepts of health or hygiene will supply a convincing explanation we should note that the early rahit-namas do display a lively sense of the perils of pollution (ritual pollution, not environmental). It may well be their understanding of pollution which supplies the essential clue to their abhorrence of hookah-smoking.

The treatment of Muslims by the early rahit-namas clearly suggests that they were regarded as polluting and in the case of the *Chaupā Singh Rahit-nāmā* the belief is explicitly stated.[31] It is quite possible that the smoking ban supplies an example of the marked hostility which the early rahit-namas show towards Muslims and all that may be associated with them. This feature is overtly expressed in the insistence that Sikhs must eat *jhatkā* meat (the flesh of an animal killed with a single blow), avoiding all contact with the *halāl* meat of the Muslims. Another prominent example is the ban on sexual contact with Muslim women (an item which a later, more sensitive generation was to transform into a prohibition of adultery). The hookah traveled eastwards with Muslims and was widely used in Muslim society. As such it may well have been regarded as a distinctively Muslim practice and thus a candidate for proscription.

The actual origins of the hostility can presumably be traced to the extended period of warfare with Muslim authorities, commencing early in the seventeenth century but fought with particular intensity during the eighteenth. Injunctions which reflect this hostility could have entered the conventional behavior of the Panth at any stage during this period. The more settled conditions of the Singh Sabha period produced a weakened emphasis on anti-Muslim features of the Rahit, a muting process which has fitfully continued through most of the present century. The events of 1947–48 fired old animosities once again, followed by a gradual subsiding of feelings; and for some at least the events of 1984 seem to have actually produced a cautious alliance between Sikhs and Muslims, each for differing reasons aimed at the central government of India.

Having thus developed a reasonably plausible explanation for the ban on hookah-smoking we must acknowledge that there are other possibilities. It might be argued that the hookah was banned because it would reduce the alertness and mobility of Khalsa guerrillas. Although the Muslim connection seems the more likely explanation, support for it must be tempered with an awareness of other options. Competing explanations serve to emphasize the complexity of the task which confronts anyone seeking to understand and explain the Rahit.

This discussion could be continued at great length, scrutinizing the many features of the traditional Rahit and seeking to explain each of them in turn. In briefly pursuing it I have touched on a second problem. A major source for understanding the evolving Rahit must obviously be the corpus of rahit-namas, supplemented by relevant references in the gur-bilas literature and other early sources. If, however, the rahit-namas are to yield useful information they must be satisfactorily located in terms of time, place and purpose. This is still impossible to do in most instances.

The problem has already been noted with regard to *Gur Sobhā*, though at least it is possible to locate that particular work to within half a century and it seems to raise no serious problems as far as the interests of its author are concerned. In the case of the *Chaupā Singh Rahit-nāmā* it is possible to proceed much further, placing it in the fifth decade of the eighteenth century and associating it with a family of disaffected Brahman Sikhs who had lost a coveted influence within the Panth (p. 19). That is a very substantial gain, and so too is the firm location of the works of Santokh Singh, author of *Nānak Prakāś* and *Sūraj Prakāś* (see chapter 6). There are many problems to be overcome when dealing with Santokh Singh, not least the difficulties presented by his Braj-influenced Punjabi. It is, however, a substantial help when seeking to interpret his work to know that he was educated within the Niramala tradition, resided in the Malwa region, and wrote during the first half of the nineteenth century.

Because of the contextual information which can be assembled with regard to the *Chaupā Singh Rahit-nāmā* and the works of Santokh Singh such sources can yield valuable returns. But what can be deduced from the remaining rahit-namas, notably the brief verse versions which have been so influential? One is bound to acknowledge that at present their effective contribution must remain limited, for none of them can yet be convincingly located in terms of author, time or purpose. Their alleged origins can easily be set aside and this is a necessary first step. The Nand Lal of Guru Gobind Singh's retinue could not possibly have produced the naive style of the rahit-namas which bear his name; and the Prahilad Singh/Rai work ends with a date which makes no sense if we are to believe the author's claims concerning the circumstances under which he recorded the Guru's words.[32] There is, moreover, no manuscript evidence to support an early origin.[33]

These and other features indicate that the verse rahit-namas must be detached from their alleged origins. It does not necessarily follow, however, that they must be separated by a substantial distance. The actual contents of these rahit-namas are generally consistent with an early stage of rahit-nama development, a conspicuous example being the absence of any clear reference to the Five Ks.[34]

The problem remains, one of the many which demand attention in the near future. Until it is solved any comprehensive conclusion must be deferred regarding the eighteenth-century development of the Rahit. Also the precise origins of some very influential words must remain unknown. Attention has already been drawn to the "rāj karegā khālsā" couplet which occurred in the *Tanakhāh-nāmā* and is recited in gurdwaras following the conclusion of Ardas (the Sikh Prayer). It would be very helpful to know when these words were first composed. The same tantalizing delay must apply to the two couplets which precede "rāj karegā khālsā" in the regular Ardas supplement. These couplets appear in an earlier form as separate parts of the Prahilad Singh/Rai rahitnama:

> *gurū khālsā mānīahi paragaṭ gurū kī deh,*
> *jo sikh mo milabo chāhahi khoj inahu mahi lehu.*

Accept the Khalsa as Guru, for it is the manifest body of the Guru. The Sikh who wishes to find me should seek me in its midst.

> *ākal purakh ke bachan siun pragaṭ chalāyo panth;*
> *sabh sikhan ko bachan hai gurū mānīahu granth.*

The Panth was founded at the command of Akal Purakh. Every Sikh is bidden to accept the Granth as Guru. [35]

It would greatly assist our understanding if we could definitively date these two couplets. [36]

In theory, of course, such problems can be regarded as merely academic. If the doctrine of the mystically-present Guru is to be accepted it must follow that the Guru's guidance continues to be given. This in turn means that there is doctrinal sanction for the notion of an ever-developing Rahit. In practice it is not so easy. It is difficult because the tradition of a fully-formed Rahit commands such enormous respect, and also because the process of interpreting the Guru's will in today's circumstances encounters such serious obstacles. This is the third problem, the question of authority within the modern Panth.

Who possesses the right to determine the proper content of the Rahit and thus to define the meaning of Sikh identity? In a general sense there is a routine answer to the question of authority in the Panth, one which few practicing Sikhs are likely to dispute. The ultimate authority is the Guru and the objective standard is the Guru Granth Sahib. This, however, returns to the doctrine of the mystically-present Guru and, as we have just noted, the doctrine is one which in practice leaves most Rahit problems unsolved. The Adi Granth provides little specific guidance on issues relating to the Rahit, and differences of opinion quickly emerge whenever the attempt is made to apply its general principles to particular cases.

Although no orthodox Sikh questions the obligation to utilize the guidance of the sacred scripture in all such issues the procedure will seldom produce clear, incontestable answers. Dependence on the individual conscience is likewise unsatisfactory as a means of determining basic principles. For certain personal decisions each individual can claim responsibility (preferably in conjunction with a reading of the Guru Granth Sahib), but not for general issues affecting the fundamental beliefs or normative practices of the Panth. The problem requires a more convincing answer, one which will involve an objective authority with an acknowledged right to deliver specific judgments.

Two different solutions can be offered, neither of them solving the problem in terms which will be acceptable to all. The first answer is that the Shiromani Gurdwara Parbandhak Committee possesses the authority to make such decisions. Democratically elected by adult Sikhs living in the Punjab and neighboring districts the SGPC stands forth as the manifest expression of the *Sarbat Khālsā* and as such it holds the Guru-given right to speak with authority on all matters of panthic concern. It is the SGPC which issues *Sikh Rahit Maryādā* and its imprimatur signals ultimate authority.

This answer will immediately prompt a number of objections. The first is that the SGPC represents, at best, only the Sikhs of its electorate. This excludes the vitally important Delhi constituency and the equally important diaspora. A second objection is that enrollment as a voter in SGPC elections depends on a prior definition of who is a Sikh, thus begging the most fundamental of questions.[37] This particular objection is further strengthened by the fact that the electoral definition requires each voter to testify that he or she abstains from alcohol.[38] Some firmly reject this item as a part of the definition of a Sikh. Others who might be prepared to include it in an ideal definition acknolwedge it to be so widely disregarded in practice as to be meaningless. A third objection for many is that the SGPC is too deeply involved in sordid politics to be acceptable as an ultimate authority for matters of faith and behavior. It may still serve a purpose as the administrator of gurdwara funds, but it is far too compromised to act as a religious court of final appeal.

The alternative is the local sangat (congregation), either as an assembly of all adherents or through powers delegated to five trusted members acting as Panj Piare. This raises another set of objections. First, who decides the qualifications for sangat membership? Secondly, who will believe that sangats are immune from the kind of political activity which, for many Sikhs, disqualifies the SGPC? Thirdly, who adjudicates the differences of interpretation which are bound to distinguish one sangat from another? The Panth would disperse into an ever-expanding array of independent congregations. Local customs would be formalized within each group and the Rahit would slip into ever-deepening confusion.

The immediate response to this prophecy of doom is that in practice it just does not happen that way. This implies the only possible answer to the problem. In practice the Panth has learnt to live with a radically uncertain theory of ultimate authority. Although the result involves constant stress there nevertheless persists a sufficient measure of agreed uniformity. The consensus may suffer some slow attrition and an occasional upset, but at least its principal features survive. A major reason for their survival is the agreed insistence that tradition delivers a well-defined model, and that no subsequent argument or decision can change that model. This in turn helps us to understand why the defense of a traditional identity is so important.

The absence of an executive authority with acknowledged powers must ensure that certain issues will continue to trouble the Panth for periods covering many decades and sometimes centuries. Some of the issues are trivial matters, but by no means all can be dismissed in this way. Reference has just been made to the requirement that all who qualify as voters in SGPC elections must swear that they are total abstainers from alcohol. Is abstinence an approved feature of the Rahit? *Sikh Rahit Maryādā* specifically declares alcohol to be an offense, but where does one find the scriptural or traditional justification for this claim?[39] Justifications do indeed exist, but all lend themselves to alternate explanations and the question remains doubtful. It is common knowledge that alcohol is copiously consumed by many members of the Panth and few of them seem inclined to apologize for the practice. Others insist that it is wrong and the issue remains undecided.

For some the debate also extends to meat-eating. In this arena it is the consumers rather than the abstainers who can claim the support of *Sikh Rahit Maryādā*, provided only that the meat is *jhaṭkā* and is not *halāl*.[40] The influence of the Indian tradition is, however, strong. It ensures that meat-eating continues to be controversial and that few of the consumers will touch beef, particularly in India.

Opinion hardens again when we return to the ban on smoking, an injunction which is widely upheld. Although the ban has moved from smoking the hookah to all forms of tobacco it remains relatively firm. Paradoxically the line drawn against smoking has held more securely than the emphatic prohibition of hair-cutting. The latter is an absolutely fundamental feature of the Rahit, one which clearly dates from the seventeenth century and which no statement of the Rahit ever overlooks. There are, however, many who claim the title of Sikh and yet cut their hair. We are finally brought to the most basic of all problems of Sikh identity, one which has been with the Panth ever since the founding of the Khalsa and which remains with it to the present day.

Strictly speaking there are two kinds of Sikhs who refrain from cutting their hair. All who observe the convention (i.e., all who retain the *kes*) are called *Kes-dhārī* Sikhs, regardless of whether or not they accept Khalsa initiation. Those who do undergo the rite of initiation (and thereby "take *amrit*") become *Amrit-dhārī* Sikhs. What this means is that *all* who retain the *kes* are Kes-dharis, and that *some* Kes-dharis are also Amrit-dharis. Although there is no means of knowing what proportion are baptized Amrit-dharis it seems clear that they constitute a relatively small minority of the total Kes-dhari constituency.

The situation becomes even more complex when we turn to those who do cut their hair, for here there are three distinct varieties to be noted. For one of the three the act technically amounts to apostasy and as such is implicitly condemned in *Sikh Rahit Maryādā*; four grievous sins (the *chār kurahit*) are specified and the initiated Sikh who commits any of them qualifies as *patit* ("fallen" or "renegade"). The first of the four offenses is, predictably, the cutting of one's hair. This means that a baptized member of the Khalsa (viz. an Amrit-dhari) who cuts his (or her) hair becomes a Patit Sikh, one who should properly be ostracized by all loyal adherents of the Khalsa until the sin has been confessed and due penance performed. This is the strictly orthodox response. In practice the level of disapproval ranges from outrage to indifference, and although some may feel strongly on the issue the word *patit* is seldom heard.

In spite of this ambivalent response *Sikh Rahit Maryādā* is relatively clear with regard to the theoretical status of the Patit Sikh. It is much less clear when dealing with the two remaining varieties of hair-cutting Sikh, although one of the two has been the subject of recurrent debate within the Panth during the past century. This is the variety known as Sahaj-dhari Sikhs. Such people will typically claim to be ardent admirers of the personal Guru and loyal devotees of the Guru Granth Sahib. Their actual observance, however, is limited to the *nām simaraṇ* teachings of Nanak and his early successors. They do not adopt the names Singh or Kaur as required by the Khalsa discipline and although they may well be devout practitioners of *nit-nem* (the daily rule) and regular visitors to the gurdwara they are certainly not Sikhs of the Khalsa. Are they truly Sikhs? If so, what is the purpose and special value of the Khalsa?

Confronted by this problem the Singh Sabha reformers (specifically the Tat Khalsa) fastened on a particular etymology of the term *sahaj-dhārī*. It seems likely that the first part of the compound originally referred to the condition of ultimate bliss as described by Guru Nanak.[41] One of the words by Nanak to describe this condition was *sahaj* and this is evidently the meaning which should properly be read into the compound *sahaj-dhārī*. Sahaj-dharis were those who sought the ineffable *sahaj-avasthā* in the manner indicated by Guru Nanak. In other words they sought to attain the bliss of *sahaj* by means of *nām simaraṇ*, without the Khalsa discipline.

Guru Nanak's usage, however, involves a specialized meaning of the word. The usual meaning of *sahaj* is "easy" or "slow," and the Singh Sabha theory was that the term *sahaj-dhārī* should be construed as "slow-adopter" or "one who proceeds by easy stages." The Sahaj-dharis were thus to be treated as aspirants to full membership of the Khalsa who had not yet attained their goal. In this manner they could theoretically be accommodated within the Khalsa ideal. They could also be accepted as loyal (if implicitly subordinate) allies of the true Khalsa.

This conclusion was uneasily accepted by the compilers of *Sikh Rahit Maryādā*, their hesitation clearly indicated by the muffled and ambiguous terms which they use. The third variety is completely ignored, though it actually poses the most serious problem of all. Patits have always been few in number and the Sahaj-dhari identity seems plainly to be in rapid decline. The same cannot be said for Sikhs who cut their hair without qualifying for either Patit or Sahaj-dhari status. These are Sikhs who belong to a category best described as "affiliated Khalsa." Those who belong to this category occupy the extensive middle ground between the formal Khalsa of the Patit Sikh and the overtly non-Khalsa of the Sahaj-dhari. Many within it retain the Kes-dhari identity. Others cut their hair without renouncing the affiliation and these are the people who constitute the third variety of hair-cutting Sikhs.

Those who belong to this group should not incur condemnation as Patits because they have never been Amrit-dharis; and because of their inherited links with the Khalsa tradition they cannot be treated as Sahaj-dharis. Many were once Kes-dharis. Others who have always cut their hair retain the link by virtue of a family tradition of loyalty to the Khalsa ideal. Sikhs of this kind are particularly numerous in countries outside India, and although recent events have slowed the trend it can be expected to quicken again when peace returns to the Punjab. No existing term describes them accurately and we must accordingly use the imprecise label of *monā* or "shaven."

As with the question of Patit status the issue is one which elicits a range of responses. For those who regard the Khalsa identity as the only acceptable answer the Mona style is altogether unacceptable. Some who adopt this strict view actually equate the Mona with the Patit, applying to both the same rigorous condemnation. Others regard the issue with uncertain embarrassment, and many more treat it with apparent unconcern. Mona Sikhs themselves usually insist that they are retaining their Sikh identity, and many of those living overseas affirm their claim by regularly attending a gurdwara. If they are Jats by caste the claim is usually an easy one to sustain. Others may find it more difficult, particularly those who belong to urban castes. In the case of the latter cutting their hair may well amount to returning to a Hindu identity.

The issue is not one that can be put aside indefinitely. Although it is unlikely to be resolved by a deliberate decision on the part of any formal authority some form of resolution is bound to emerge, one which will reflect the increasing influence of Sikhs living overseas. Actual practice will determine what votes and decrees can never achieve. This should not imply an inevitable dismantling of the orthodox Khalsa identity, a mistaken conclusion which was drawn by many British observers a century ago. Much depends on the accident of future events and the pressures which they will impose on the Panth.

One final issue may be briefly noted. Whenever meetings are held to discuss the present circumstances and future prospects of the Panth the subject of caste is commonly raised, particularly if there are articulate young Sikhs present. Here too alien circumstances place much greater strains on many diaspora Sikhs, but it is a topic of frequent comment wherever Sikhs discuss the nature of their faith and practice. The situation seems to involve a clear contradiction between the teachings of the Gurus on the one hand and the practice of the Panth on the other. Whereas the Gurus affirm equality and condemn caste the actual practice of the Panth denies their clear purpose. In terms of ritual and dining customs the injunction to spurn caste is generally observed, although caste gurdwaras are by no means unknown. When it comes to marriage arrangements, however, the old conventions seem to stand as firm as ever.

There are two possible solutions to this problem. One is to persist in the belief that caste is wrong and endeavor to breach the marital barrier. For most this will not be easy in present circumstances and such hopes may well prove to be illusory. It may, however, succeed as circumstances change and it may actually be forced on many groups of diaspora Sikhs.

The second option is to accept that caste in a certain sense can be a sound convention and that loyalty to the Gurus actually demands this response. It should be remembered that the Gurus arranged marriages for their own children which were in complete conformity with traditional caste prescription. Does it not follow therefore that their strictures on caste have been partially misunderstood? Was it not the discriminatory aspect of caste to which they objected, the notion that some are purer that others and that access to spiritual freedom was dependent on one's place in the traditional hierarchy? In the gurdwara Sikhs are obliged to renounce caste, but need they carry this obligation into all aspects of their life? Shorn of its concern with privilege and pollution caste can be accepted as a valued social stablizer, one which ideally retains notions of place without necessarily involving degrees of status.[42]

Once again the discussion has become one of ideal types and this may perhaps serve as a reminder that for many people (including many Sikhs) the question "Who is a Sikh?" is not really an important one. Who really cares, apart from the pious and the academic? Most Sikhs know that they are Sikhs without requiring a detailed analysis of the Rahit.

That sort of response is sufficient for most people most of the time. In a time of crisis, however, it may prove to be a thoroughly inadequate answer and we should need little reminding that crisis is indeed the present experience of the Panth. An adequate answer can scarcely be expected from those who stand outside the tradition. They may ask sympathetic questions and probe the initial responses which they receive, but the answer is not theirs to give. It can come only from within the Panth and it can never be a final one. Changing circumstances will ensure that the question "Who is a Sikh?" must forever be asked and never definitively answered.

6

The Literature
of the Sikhs

WHENEVER the question of Sikh literature is raised one automatically thinks of the Adi Granth. This is entirely natural. The sacred volume is of crucial importance in the Panth, revered as no other Sikh scripture is revered and regarded as an authority which none may question. As such it inevitably dominates any discussion of Sikh literature and this will be true of the treatment which follows. Having acknowledged its primacy, however, I shall endeavor to curtail the discussion and turn to other works of importance in the field of Sikh literature. This procedure will be adopted because detailed accounts of the Adi Granth already exist.[1] Descriptions and analyses of supplementary Sikh literature are, by contrast, much more sparse and there is a danger that its importance will remain largely unrecognized.

In addition to the Adi Granth we shall accordingly examine the Dasam Granth, the works of Bhai Gurdas and Bhai Nand Lal, the janam-sakhis, the gur-bilas literature, and some of the works which were produced by the Singh Sabha movement. A complete survey would also include the rahit-namas, but because they have already been described in the last chapter they will be omitted from this one.

The Adi Granth may be viewed from many different perspectives. It occupies a position of great significance in the early development of the Panth, serving as the principal repository of the Gurus' doctrine and also an important symbol of the Panth's emergent identity. In the modern context it also serves a key purpose in terms of ritual, occupying the central position in all Sikh ceremonies. This role it fulfills not merely because it is the primary scripture but more particularly because it is believed to embody, in a strictly literal sense, the eternal Guru. It is the "manifest body of the Guru" and as such it is treated with the most profound respect. In such circumstances one normally abandons the term "Adi Granth." It is the "Guru Granth Sahib" which thus receives the veneration of all Sikhs, the Granth or book which incarnates the actual presence of the Guru.

We return to the title Adi Granth when we approach the volume as students rather than as devotees. The distinction is a useful one, for whereas "Adi Granth" is a neutral title "Guru Granth" or "Guru Granth Sahib" imply a confession of faith. Adi means simply "first" or "original" and has been used to distinguish the volume compiled by Guru Arjan from the later Dasam Granth. For historians, philologists and theologians it is a treasure-house which has yet to yield the full store of its riches. In the areas which concern scholars of these disciplines its resources have been little tapped, a neglect which can be attributed to a variety of reasons. To some extent it may be an ignorance of the richness of its contents. It may also derive from an exaggerated fear of the difficulties which will be encountered, or perhaps from an inadequate recognition of the Panth's importance. There are indeed some major difficulties associated with the text of the Adi Granth, but they are certainly not problems which should inhibit attempts to analyze its language or trace the doctrinal developments which it presents.

The history of the Adi Granth is relatively clear as far as its origins are concerned, but unclear with regard to the subsequent history of the original manuscript. According to well-founded tradition the original version was recorded by the famous disciple Bhai Gurdas, acting as amanuensis for Guru Arjan.[2] The task was performed in Amritsar over a period extending from 1603 into 1604. As a major source for his new scripture Guru Arjan is said to have used an earlier collection compiled for Guru Amar Das (the so-called Goindval *pothīs*). During the seventeenth and eighteenth centuries, however, the actual location and treatment of the manuscript is obscure. Tradition maintains that it was stolen by Dhir Mal, the grandson of Guru Hargobind and a disappointed aspirant to the succession. Guru Gobind Singh subsequently asked for it to be returned to the legitimate Guru and when his request was refused he is said to have produced his own copy by dictating the entire contents from memory. To the original text he added compositions by his father, the martyred Guru Tegh Bahadur, and perhaps a couplet of his own.[3]

If the tradition is to be believed it means that the later recension containing the works of the ninth Guru was thus created by Guru Gobind Singh. The original version is known as the Kartarpur *bīr* ("volume" or "recension"), so-called because Dhir Mal and his successors lived in the small town of Kartarpur near Jalandhar. The version attributed to Guru Gobind Singh is called the Damdama *bīr*. A third recension is the Banno version which tradition locates chronologically between the other two. Tradition stoutly upholds the claims of the concordant Kartarpur and Damdama versions, rejecting Banno with equal firmness. Because of its deviant reputation the latter is also known as the *kharī bīr* (the "brackish" or "spurious" version). An alternative explanation derives the name from Khara, the village from which Banno is said to have come.

Damdama apparently agrees with Kartarpur in all respects, adding only the compositions of Guru Tegh Bahadur and the couplet which may perhaps be the work of Guru Gobind Singh. As such it is accepted as the "authorized" version and printed editions reproduce its received text. Banno, diverging from the other two, incorporates additional material which the "orthodox" recensions lack.[4] This difference raises a problem which must be discussed later.

Although the Banno version raises a serious textual problem it does nothing to disrupt the remarkably consistent structure of the Adi Granth. When Guru Arjan dictated his scripture to Bhai Gurdas he followed a well-defined pattern, conferring on the collection a regular organization which is seldom breached. The Adi Granth begins with an introductory section containing works which serve a liturgical purpose; and it concludes with an epilogue comprising a group of miscellaneous works which evidently failed to find a place in the middle section. It is this middle section which supplies both the bulk of the collection's contents (more than ninety percent of the total) and also its distinctive structure.

The basic division of the middle section of the Adi Granth is into ragas or metrical modes (a total of thirty-one). Each raga is then sub-divided according to the length of compositions, working from the shorter variety of hymn to the longer. Each of these classifications is further subdivided according to author, the hymns of Guru Nanak coming first and those of Guru Arjan appearing last. Works attributed to authors other than the Gurus (the so-called Bhagats) are grouped at the end of each raga. Amongst the Bhagats of the Adi Granth the most prominent figure is Kabir, followed by Namdev, Ravidas (Raidas), and various other poets whose works match the doctrinal concerns of Guru Arjan. The Adi Granth thus provides one of the major collections of Sant works and significant use has been made of its Kabir material by scholars interested in the development of the Kabirian tradition.[5]

In terms of language the Adi Granth presents an interesting variety, one which predictably covers a range of linguistic usage but which nevertheless sustains a sufficient degree of uniformity to justify the use of a single collective term. Christopher Shackle cautiously labels this collective "the Sacred Language of the Sikhs" (SLS). In so doing he stresses the "mixed character" of the Adi Granth language, a result of drawing on "a variety of local languages and dialects, as well as incorporating a good many archaic forms and words."[6] Elsewhere, however, he identifies a linguistic pattern which is sufficiently consistent to permit a simple diagram.[7]

This diagram should be viewed in geographical terms, with Professor Shackle's football seen as covering the Punjab. The football designates the "core" and substantial bulk of the collection, with only minor supplements represented in the three outliers. Within the core the thick arrows mark a progressive development in historical as well as geographical (or geo-linguistic) terms. Beginning with the Punjabi of Guru Nanak's *Japuji* it progresses through the Western Hindi of Guru Arjan's *Sukhmani*, eventually reaching the Braj of Guru Tegh Bahadur. The period covered extends from the beginning of the sixteenth century (Guru Nanak) through to the beginning of the seventeenth century (Guru Arjan), and onwards to the middle of the same century (Guru Tegh Bahadur).

Although this period of development covers one and a half centuries all but the last contribution (a very small one) falls within a single century and a comparatively narrow linguistic range. As such it represents a Punjabi/Western Hindi version of Sant Bhasa, the "language of the

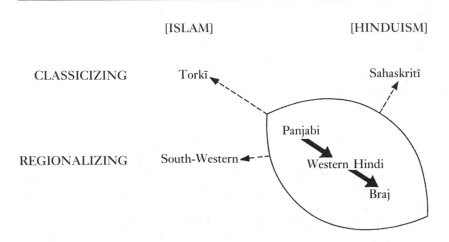

The linguistic pattern of the Adi Granth

Sants." Sant Bhasa (also known as Sadhukari) served as a lingua franca for the Sant tradition from which Gurmat emerged.[8] There is, in other words, a significant degree of linguistic uniformity within the Adi Granth, one which covers the works of the Bhagats as well as those of the Gurus. Anyone who knows the Gurmukhi script and has learnt to read Sant Bhasa should have little difficulty in understanding most of the Adi Granth.[9]

The three tiny outliers represented in Professor Shackle's diagram are interesting for their content as well as their language. Torki (Indo-Persian) and South-Western (Multani) forms are used when Muslim doctrines are invoked or a Muslim audience is addressed. The first of these linguistic usages involves an appeal to a classical ideal and so too does the third outlier. In the case of Sahaskriti, however, it is the Hindu tradition which is addressed.[10] The core takes its place within the grid established by the outliers. It is much closer to Hindu tradition than to Islam and in linguistic terms it occupies a regional location.

The linguistic pattern identified by Professor Shackle is also highly suggestive with regard to the doctrines of the Adi Granth. Here too we encounter diversity within a generally consistent frame. It is a diversity which develops as one Guru succeeds another, yet without any suggestion that a later Guru has transgressed the bounds set by his predecessors. As we have already seen, the fundamental message of Guru

Nanak is that liberation can be achieved only through meditation on the divine Name. This remains the message of all the Gurus whose works appear in the Adi Granth, but if we limit ourselves to this single statement we shall do them serious injustice with regard to the diversity which they present.

The diverse styles offered by Nanak's successors range from Guru Angad's pithy couplets and the eminently simple declarations of Guru Amar Das to the music of Guru Ram Das. Most prolific of all the Gurus, Arjan covers a wide span of human experience and related doctrine. In marked contrast Guru Tegh Bahadur stresses the theme of suffering and the imminence of death.[11] The Adi Granth is both one and many. On the one hand there is little that fails to fit a single, consistent doctrinal pattern. On the other there is a variety which serves to stress and illuminate different aspects of the pattern. It is a pattern which will be very familiar to those who are acquainted with Sant doctrine, and it offers an exposition of that doctrine which no other collection can match.[12]

The doctrinal consistency of the Adi Granth is, like the beauty of so much of its poetry, something that neither the textual problems nor neglect can destroy. There are, however, two textual problems which should be noted, and likewise two varieties of neglect. Although the two textual problems deserve close scrutiny they will not receive it here, mainly because there is little progress to report on descriptions of both problems which were published more than a decade ago. I shall accordingly limit myself to brief notices of these two textual issues.[13]

The first issue concerns the existence of the two Goindval *pothīs* and (if in fact the two volumes did exist) the extent to which they were used in compiling the Adi Granth. The claim that Guru Arjan had access to such a source is entirely plausible and arguably the compiling of the Adi Granth becomes much harder to understand if we dismiss it. The tradition which describes the origin of the *pothīs* during the time of Guru Amar Das is likewise plausible and to some extent it is supported by claims that the actual volumes still exist.[14] By itself, however, a plausible tradition is inadequate. The reliability of the tradition needs to be examined and if the artifacts actually exist they should be brought to light and duly analyzed. Neither need has been met in the case of the Goindval *pothīs* and until both tasks have been satisfactorily performed the tradition must be regarded with some skepticism.

The second issue is also stalled and no progress will be possible until scholars secure access to the manuscript in Kartarpur which tradition holds to be the document actually written by Bhai Gurdas. The manuscript, as we have already noted, disappeared during the seventeenth century. In 1849 the annexing British discovered in the custody of the Lahore court a manuscript which was identified as the Bhai Gurdas original. The large *pothī* had evidently been delivered to Lahore in 1830 by the successor of Dhir Mal, and having been satisfied that Dhir Mal's descendants were indeed its legitimate owners the British restored the manuscript to Kartarpur.[15] Carefully guarded by the Kartarpur family it has remained unexamined ever since, apart from a period of brief access which occurred in the mid-1940s while its ownership was subject to litigation.[16] The volume is displayed once a month for the purposes of *darśan*, but actual examination of the text is not permitted.

A textual problem of considerable significance is indicated by a comparison of the Banno recension with reports concerning the actual contents of the Kartarpur manuscript. This comparison suggests that the Banno recension may actually represent the original text inscribed by Bhai Gurdas. The theory allows that the Kartarpur manuscript may well be the document recorded by Bhai Gurdas, but adds that if this is indeed the case the original version has subsequently been amended by obliterating occasional portions of the text. The evidence for this hypothesis is by no means overwhelming, but a prima facie case for investigation certainly exists.[17] Until the Kartarpur manuscript can be properly examined the inquiry must be postponed.

The two varieties of neglect also require little comment. One already indicated in passing is the notable lack of attention which the Adi Granth has received from scholars outside the Punjab and from university teachers responsible for courses dealing with sacred texts. The second may perhaps seem more surprising. Within the Panth itself knowledge of the actual contents of the Adi Granth is very limited. In overseas communities where Punjabi is beginning to give way to English as the primary language of communication this feature is becoming even more pronounced.

This should certainly not suggest, however, that reverence for the sacred volume is showing any sign of diminishing. It remains the "manifest body of the Guru" and as such it continues to receive appropriate gestures of devout respect. Strictly speaking its mere presence transforms a room or building into a gurdwara and certainly no gurdwara will be without at least one large copy, reverently wrapped in expensive cloth and installed under a canopy. All who enter a gurdwara are expected to touch the floor with their foreheads before the sacred volume, and none may sit on a level higher than the lectern on which it is placed. At appropriate times during a service of worship hymns are read from the book with great reverence, the actual pages meanwhile being protected from contamination by means of a whisk. Most of the remainder of a regular service consists of kirtan (the singing of hymns from the same scripture). In a gurdwara it is customary for kirtan to be led by a group of three singers (*rāgīs*), with other members of the sangat joining in the singing as they feel inclined.[18]

The Guru Granth Sahib also occupies the central position in other Sikh rituals. If specific guidance is required for any purpose the sacred volume should be opened at random and the first hymn beginning on the left-hand page should be read for whatever help it may give. When a child is to be named the volume is similarly opened at random and the name which is chosen should begin with the same letter as the first hymn on the randomly-chosen left page. A wedding conducted in accordance with the Anand rite must take place in the presence of the Guru Granth Sahib and the actual marriage is performed by having the couple walk around the volume four times. A funeral should be accompanied by the singing of hymns from the Guru Granth Sahib and followed by a complete reading of the entire scripture.[19]

Complete readings of the Guru Granth Sahib are a prominent feature of the Panth's life, performing a valuable social function while emphasizing the importance of the sacred scripture as a key denominator of the Panth's identity. For special occasions an "unbroken reading" (*akhaṇḍ pāṭh*) will be conducted by a relay of readers, a task which occupies approximately forty-eight hours.[20] Complete readings may also be spread over longer periods, as little as a week or as much as a year. Such readings (*sādhāran pāṭh*) are held to mark occasions of grief or joy, or in order to secure divine favor for a particular undertaking. Relatives, friends and acquaintances are commonly invited to be present during the *bhog* ceremony with which the complete reading concludes, particularly in the case of an *akhaṇḍ pāṭh*.[21]

The Adi Granth is the Guru and as such it receives the honor and reverence which the personal Gurus would have received from their Sikhs. During the eighteenth century the same respect was also bestowed on the second of the Sikh scriptures, the Dasam Granth. It too was regarded as the visibly present Guru and thus received the same veneration.[22] That veneration has now diminished in the case of the Dasam Granth and although it still ranks as a sacred scripture few Sikhs would place the entire collection on the same level as the Adi Granth. Supreme honor of that order is reserved for only a few portions of the Dasam Granth, not the volume as a whole. Certain works attributed to Guru Gobind Singh are treated with the same respect as the *bāṇī* of the Adi Granth, but the Dasam Granth as a whole is seldom invoked and little understood.

The Dasam Granth is a substantial work comprising 1,428 pages in its printed edition. Within the collection four varieties of composition may be distinguished. The first group comprises two works which may be regarded as autobiographical or at least as biographical, both of them attributed to Guru Gobind Singh. These are *Bachitar Nāṭak* or "The Wondrous Drama" (an account of the Guru's previous incarnation, early life, and battles with his neighbors in the Shivalik Hills) and *Zafar-nāmā* (a defiant letter addressed to the Emperor Aurangzeb). The second cluster consists of four devotional works attributed to Guru Gobind Singh (*Jāp, Akāl Ustat, Giān Prabodh*, and *Śabad Hazāre*). The third comprises two miscellaneous works (*Savayye* and *Śastar nām-mālā*); and the fourth a collection of legendary narratives and popular anecdotes. It is this fourth group which constitutes the bulk of the Dasam Granth (more than eighty percent of the total). Like most of the remainder the works in this section are written in Braj, one of the reasons which explains the general neglect of the Dasam Granth.[23]

Research on the Dasam Granth has been very limited, with the result that most of the major questions which it raises cannot be answered at present. These questions commence with the problem of its actual origins and indeed with the very name which it bears. Most continue to assume that it must mean "The Book of the Tenth [Guru]," but some claim that it should be construed as "The Tenth Portion" of a much larger work.[24]

Four theories are current concerning the origins of the Dasam Granth. The traditional view is that the entire collection is the work of Guru Gobind Singh himself. A second theory is that the first three clusters may be attributed to Guru Gobind Singh, but that the remainder must have been the work of writers who belonged to his retinue.[25] A third interpretation maintains that nothing except *Zafar-nāmā* can be safely attributed to Guru Gobind Singh. This interpretation agrees that the collection derives from the following attracted by the Guru, but that it should be read as a reflection of ideas and attitudes rather than as a source for his "authentic" compositions. A fourth theory agrees that only *Zafar-nāmā* has strong claims to authenticity, but restricts the remainder of the third interpretation to the first three varieties of composition. The legendary narratives and popular anecdotes obviously had a clientele within the Panth, but they need not be interpreted as works which reflect the ideals and attitudes of the Guru himself.[26]

At this stage it is quite impossible to evaluate these four theories adequately. There is now little support for the first theory except in the popular imagination; and it may be noted that although the second is still plausible it has been seriously weakened by a recent analysis of *Bachitar Nāṭak*.[27] The essential analysis, however, still remains to be done and until it is done it will be impossible to affirm any of the contending theories with assurance.

As far as the ongoing life of the Panth is concerned such issues are perhaps irrelevant and this is presumably the conclusion which we should draw from the neglect which the Dasam Granth receives. *Jāp Sāhib* and the *Savayye Amrit* are firmly lodged in the regular pattern of daily devotions (*nit-nem*). *Akāl Ustat* offers some magnificent poetry, *Bachitar Nāṭak* helps us to understand the Guru's early wars, and *Zafar-nāmā* dramatically expresses his defiance. The remainder is, in effect, discarded and some potentially embarrassing questions are thereby avoided. Difficult questions are bound to be raised if the bulk of the Dasam Granth is carefully examined, for the kind of Puranic material which dominates the narrative and anecdotal portion of the Dasam Granth is scarcely consonant with the preferred interpretation of the Sikh tradition.

This policy may be explicable, but the neglect which it sustains is unfortunate. Locked within the Dasam Granth is an understanding of the early Khalsa which at present is lacking. Although this understanding will not yield to a mere reading of the volume's various contents it must assuredly emerge from their careful analysis. It cannot be claimed that the Dasam Granth alone will answer every question. This assuredly it will not do. With equal certainty, however, an analysis of its contents will insistently raise many of the issues associated with the early development of the Khalsa, and any successful attempt to grapple with these issues will significantly advance understanding of the evolving Panth. The task is a forbidding one, demanding a language background which few possess together with analytical skills of a high order.

It will be an exceedingly hard nut to crack, but cracked it must be if there is to be an adequate understanding of the crucial period covering the late seventeenth and early eighteenth centuries.

The Adi Granth occupies the supreme position in terms of sanctity, and if the Dasam Granth is to be accorded its traditional status it should be treated as an equal. In practice this is not the case, except in gurdwaras managed by the Nihang Sikhs.[28] The Dasam Granth may nevertheless be installed and read in gurdwaras, and if not the actual equal of the Adi Granth it must nevertheless be treated as sacred scripture.[29]

Occupying a third level on the sacred literature scale come two collections which offer none of the ambiguities associated with the Dasam Granth. These are the works of the two distinguished Sikhs of the Guru period, Bhai Gurdas and Bhai Nand Lal. Neither collection ranks as sacred scripture in the manner of the Adi Granth or (in theory) the Dasam Granth. Both, however, are explicitly approved for recitation in gurdwaras and as such they constitute a part of what we may regard as an authorized Sikh canon.[30]

Bhai Gurdas, the earlier of the two writers, was a relative of the third Guru and closely associated with all subsequent Gurus until his death in about 1633. Although his name was Gurdas Bhalla he received the honorific title "Bhai" (Brother) and ever since he has been invariably known as Bhai Gurdas. As we have already noted, it was he whom Guru Arjan chose to act as his amanuensis during the original recording of the Adi Granth text. He was also a missionary and trusted assistant, serving his Masters in a variety of responsibilities. Most significantly he was a poet and a theologian, leaving a corpus of works which tradition regards as "the key to the Guru Granth Sahib."

There are two distinct collections within the works of Bhai Gurdas. Writing in Braj he produced a series of 556 poems in the *kabitt* style, little read for the same linguistic reason as the Dasam Granth.[31] Much more influential are his thirty-nine lengthy poems called *vārs*. These also present problems, for their Punjabi has inevitably dated and most readers require a glossary to assist in their full understanding.[32] The attempt is well worth the effort. In addition to their beauty of expression the vars contain much information concerning the life and beliefs of the early Panth. As such they provide an extensive commentary on the teaching of the Gurus, together with source material which can be very useful to the historian of the Panth. This latter feature is well illustrated by a famous stanza from Var 26, one which contrasts the differing policies and life-styles of the sixth Guru and his predecessors:

> The earlier Gurus sat peaceably in dharamsalas;
> this one roams the land.
> Emperors visited their homes with reverence;
> this one they cast into prison.
> No rest for his followers, ever active;
> their restless Master has fear of none.
> The earlier Gurus sat graciously blessing;
> this one goes hunting with dogs.
> They had servants who harbored no malice;
> this one encourages scoundrels.
> Yet none of these changes conceals the truth;
> the Sikhs are still drawn as bees to the lotus.
> The truth stands firm, eternal, changeless;
> and pride still lies subdued.[33]

Here we find reflected the criticisms which Guru Hargobind evidently attracted (represented in the first five lines of the stanza) followed by the devout response of the loyal follower (the two remaining lines). If one should need evidence of the change which took place under the sixth Guru this stanza should certainly offer a contribution.

Other portions deal with the essential doctrines taught by the Gurus. In the following stanza external observances are gently yet effectively mocked:

> If bathing at tiraths procures liberation frogs,
> for sure, must be saved;
> And likewise the banyan with tangling tresses,
> if growing hair long sets one free.
> If the need can be served by roaming unclad
> the deer of the forest must surely be pious;
> So too the donkey which rolls in the dust
> if limbs caked with ashes can purchase salvation.
> Saved are the cattle, mute in the field,
> if silence produces deliverance.
> Only the Guru can bring liberation;
> only the Guru can set a man free.[34]

The way of life to be followed by the devout Sikh is described in stanzas such as the following:

Rise from sleep during night's last watch
and discharge the disciple's threefold task.
Speak with courtesy, walk in humility,
practise virtue by aiding others.
Obey the Guru by acting with restraint;
sleeping, eating, speaking in moderation.
Live by your labour, performing honest toil;
never take pride in status or achievement.
Daily join with the company of the faithful,
singing God's praises by day and by night.
Seek your joy in the Guru's Word,
the means whereby he delights the soul.
Abandon the ties of wordly concern;
let your only hope be the Guru's grace.[35]

In practice Bhai Gurdas, though deeply respected within the Panth, is seldom read or heard. The same applies to Nand Lal Goya who, because he wrote in Persian, is even less accessible to most members of the Panth.[36] Although Nand Lal belonged to the retinue of Guru Gobind Singh his poems breathe a spirit very different from the militant piety which we usually associate with the tenth Guru. This may perhaps explain why his works do not appear in the Dasam Granth. In terms of both spirit and doctrine they are much more in harmony with the divine Name teachings of the earlier Gurus and it may perhaps be significant that Nand Lal's name indicates an unwillingness to adopt the Khalsa identity. His two famous works are his *Dīvān* (a collection of sixty-one *ghazals*) and his *Zindagī-nāmā*. The introductory *ghazal* of the *Dīvān* illustrates his characteristic style:

Only the longing to worship God has brought me into the world;
But for the joy of offering praise why should I ever come?
Happy the life of the man who spends his days in remembering
God;
Without that remembrance why should we linger,
under the dome of Heaven?
Without that remembrance life is death,
remembrance alone can sustain me.
Without that remembrance all that life offers
is empty and futile for me.
All that I am, my heart, my life, I offer in humble abasement,

Taking the dust from the blessed feet of the one
who has led me to you.
No trace of you had I ever seen in Heaven above
or on earth below
Until the desire to behold you, Lord, laid me prostrate
in awe and devotion.
Without the remembrance of God, O Goya, how can I ever live?
Grant that deliverance soon may be mine,
that freed I may meet my Beloved.[37]

This is far removed from the spirit and style of the early Khalsa. It is
in fact a generously open style, one with which the followers of many
different traditions would easily identify.

The same openness is also provided by the janam-sakhis, the traditional narratives of the life of Guru Nanak.[38] Although it is impossible
to say when the janam-sakhi form first developed within the Panth it
can be safely assumed that anecdotes concerning Baba Nanak would
have started to circulate as soon as his reputation began to develop and
spread. The process is a natural one and story cycles of this kind were
already a part of Punjabi culture. In the Punjab anecdotes and anecdotal
sequences were particularly associated with Sufi pirs and the janam-
sakhi narrators obviously use the Sufi style as a model. Some of the
individual stories which we find in the janam-sakhis were borrowed
directly from the Sufi store, with only the name of the central character
and some relevant details changed.[39] The actual form itself also resem-
bled the Sufi model, with several anecdotes assembled to form a coherent sequence.

This was the process which produced the janam-sakhi form within
the early Panth. Isolated anecdotes which circulated orally were evidently drawn together to constitute a rudimentary life-story, beginning
with an auspicious birth and proceeding through the various stages of
the Guru's life to his triumphant death. The sequence thus established
grew and diversified. Eventually it produced several distinct cycles or
traditions, each with its own distinctive pattern and doctrinal concerns.

At some point (probably during the early seventeenth century) there
began the practice of committing particular collections to writing, thus
enabling us to trace their development more precisely. The earliest extant manuscript is dated S.1715 (A.D. 1658) and subsequent manuscripts carry the style through to the middle of the nineteenth century.

With the arrival of the British came the printing press and during the next half-century the stock of recorded anecdotes, stimulated by the new technology, expanded dramatically. This expansion dwindled during the twentieth century and although the janam-sakhi stories continue to be very popular there is now little sign of continuing growth.

At least six traditions or distinctive sequences can be recognized.[40] The earliest extant manuscript records a version of the *Bālā* tradition, so-called because it purports to be the work of a certain Bhai Bala who (according to this tradition) was a regular companion of Guru Nanak during his travels. During the past century the *Bālā* tradition has established a firm grip and it still dominates both the book market and the popular imagination. It is clear, however, that it was not the first tradition to emerge and ironically its original version was distinctly hostile to the legitimate line of Gurus.

Throughout the present century the principal challenge to *Bālā* dominance has come from the *Purātan* tradition, a structured collection of anecdotes much favored by the Singh Sabha reformers and used by Macauliffe to supplement the framework for his life of Nanak. This tradition, which nowhere mentions Bhai Bala, was more acceptable to Macauliffe and his Singh Sabha associates, partly because it provided a more coherent sequence and partly because its miracle stories were rather less grotesque than those of the *Bālā* cycles. Just as *Bālā* has a firm hold on the popular imagination, so *Purātan* dominates the writing of respectable "biographies." It is useful to know that when we read a standard account of the life of Nanak we are reading a version which derives its shape and much of its substance from the *Purātan* tradition. *Purātan* provides a more rational account of the Guru's life, though this need not mean that it is any closer to the actual events of his life than its *Bālā* competitor.[41]

The *Purātan* tradition can be regarded as "orthodox" in its presentation of the Guru's life-story and this doubtless helped to establish its credentials for the Singh Sabha writers and their successors. The same can also be said for the *Ādi Sākhīs* tradition, but the bulky *Miharbān Janam-sākhī* is associated with the schismatic Mina sect and as such it has always been regarded with suspicion. Evidence has recently been produced to show that the *Gyān-ratanāvalī*, a janam-sakhi attributed to the celebrated eighteenth-century martyr Mani Singh, is in fact a product of the Udasi sect dating from the early nineteenth century.[42] These origins can be significant, but they normally do little to affect the actual style of the typical janam-sakhi.[43] This style can be illustrated by a brief anecdote from the composite collection known as the *B40 Janam-sākhī:*

Baba Nanak, having left that place, traveled to another country. There he came to a city where he noticed four pennants fluttering over a house. When he asked for an explanation the people told him that they marked the residence of a wealthy money-lender. "He has a large hoard of treasure which he keeps in four coffers," they said. "The four flags signify the four coffers."

Baba Nanak then approached the money-lender and asked him to explain his pennants. "The treasure which they signify will accompany me when I die," the money-lender assured him. In response Baba Nanak gave him a needle and asked him to return it when they both reached Heaven.

The money-lender accepted the needle, but later he began to worry. "How can I take this needle with me when I die?" he asked himself. "How will I be able to return it to that faqir?" He ran after Baba Nanak and having caught up with him he returned the needle. "There is no sense in my keeping it," he said.

"If there is no sense in keeping this needle," answered Baba Nanak, "how will you be able to take your four treasure-chests with you when you die?" Instantly the money-lender realized the truth and reverently begged forgiveness. He returned to his house and having given away all his possessions he applied himself to the devotional discipline which Baba Nanak taught. He became a Sikh and, liberated by the Guru's grace from the bonds of transmigration, he found true happiness.[44]

This story illustrates several of the typical features of a janam-sakhi anecdote. Baba Nanak visits a particular place during his travels and there encounters a benighted individual or some representative of conventional religion. A discussion takes place, climaxed by a symbolic gesture or a miracle. Conversion follows, the new disciple begins to practice *nām simaran*, and Baba Nanak continues on his way.

As transmitters of Nanak-panthi doctrine and convention the janam-sakhis have few rivals. In that most accessible of all forms (the simple, interesting, easily-comprehended anecdote) they repeatedly present Nanak as the Supreme Guru and his message of *nām simaran* as the one effective means of deliverance. Although they have never been accepted as sacred scripture their immense popularity has conferred on them a major role in the sustaining and transmission of the Nanak-panthi tradition.[45]

It will be noted that in thus summarizing the significance of the janam-sakhis we have specifically referred to the Nanak-panthi tradition rather than to Sikh tradition in general. The distinction is required because the latter must take account of the Khalsa transformation and in this the janam-sakhis play no part. For the Khalsa inheritance we must look elsewhere. The rahit-namas provide us with one such source. The other is the mode of historical presentation known as gur-bilas.[46]

The term *gur-bilās* means "pleasure of the Guru" and in a strictly literal sense it might well be applied to the janam-sakhis. In practice, however, it designates works which narrate the later history of the Panth in a style molded by the militant aspirations of the Khalsa. It is, in other words, a "heroic" style which emerges from the heroic period of Sikh history. Predictably its products concentrate on Guru Hargobind and (with particular emphasis) on Guru Gobind Singh. These were the two warrior Gurus, exemplifying in their own lives the ideals which were to inform the eighteenth-century Khalsa. The gur-bilas literature reflects these ideals and delivers a version of Sikh history which conspicuously embodies them.

The earliest work which can be regarded as a representative of the gur-bilas style is *Bachitar Nāṭak*, the account of the early life of Guru Gobind Singh which appears in the Dasam Granth. Because this narrative poem is traditionally attributed to Guru Gobind Singh himself it is not usually treated as an example of the "pleasure of the Guru" style. It does, however, breathe the authentic gur-bilas spirit, particularly those portions which exalt the sword or describe the early battles fought by Guru Gobind Singh.[47] It seems likely that *Bachitar Nāṭak* was the work of a close disciple rather than the Guru himself[48] and if this is correct the poem can certainly be regarded as the first of the breed.

The next to appear was Sainapati's *Gur Śobhā* or "Radiance of the Guru," variously dated 1711 and 1745. In this work particular emphasis is laid on the role and divine authority of the Khalsa. A lengthy pause followed the composing of *Gur Śobhā*. Although chronic warfare greatly strengthened the Khalsa spirit and thus the gur-bilas impulse it also inhibited the actual production of literary work. The next example of the tradition is Sukha Singh's *Gur-bilās Dasvīn Pātaśāhī*, a heroic account of the life of Guru Gobind Singh which was completed in 1797. Two other examples of the tradition which also claim eighteenth-century origins are Koer Singh's *Gur-bilās Pātaśāhī 10*, and *Gur-bilās Chhevīn Pātaśāhī* attributed to a poet called Sohan. It appears, however, that both belong to the early nineteenth century.[49]

It was the period before the middle of the nineteenth century which produced the most famous of all gur-bilas histories. This was Ratan Singh Bhangu's *Prāchīn Panth Prakāś*, completed in 1841. Also within this same period there appeared the enormously influential *Sūraj Prakāś* of Santokh Singh. In his earlier *Nānak Prakāś* Santokh Singh had followed the janam-sakhi style and this carries over to his accounts of the remaining Gurus in *Sūraj Prakāś*. The treatment is nevertheless influenced by gur-bilas ideals and as such provides an interesting blend of the two approaches, a combination which dominates much of the literature subsequently produced within the Panth.[50]

Arguably it is this same mingling of styles which appears in the works of Gian Singh, last of the traditional historians to exercise a significant influence on the received version of Sikh tradition. Gian Singh published his *Panth Prakāś* in 1880, and installments of his *Tavarīkh Gurū Khālsā* (History of the Guru Khalsa) were issued between 1891 and 1919. In these works, however, the stress has returned to the gur-bilas interpretation and Gian Singh may appropriately be regarded as its last great exemplar.[51]

By the time of Gian Singh the period of the Singh Sabha movement has arrived and with it another significant development in the literature of the Sikhs. The Singh Sabha, as indicated earlier, was a reform movement dedicated to the restoration of traditional Sikh values following a period of apparent decay. A significant role was assigned to literature, for many of the Singh Sabha leaders were educated men who believed in the power of the printed word.[52]

The Singh Sabha writers were in fact men who had been greatly influenced by the British presence in the Punjab, a presence which soon delivered the technology for disseminating literature while progressively affecting the outlook of those responsible for its production. This did not mean widespread abandoning of traditional beliefs and attitudes. The traditions were loyally retained, but they were subjected to reinterpretation in accordance with ideals exposed to the scientific and rationalist influence of Western education. The result was a restatement of traditional beliefs, one which resolutely affirmed the mission of the

Gurus but did so in terms congenial to a generation enlightened by contemporary notions of reason.

For Western readers the principal product of the movement has been M. A. Macauliffe's *The Sikh Religion*, probably followed by Teja Singh's *Sikhism: Its Ideals and Institutions*. The principal impact, however, has been felt within the Panth. First to emerge to prominence was the prolific Giani Dit Singh, a leading member of the Lahore Singh Sabha and himself a Sikh of outcaste birth.[53] Dit Singh's booklets and pamphlets were later followed by the weightier works of men such as Vir Singh, Kahn Singh Nabha, and various lesser luminaries. Meanwhile newspapers and journals were developing a marked influence on literate Sikhs. These publications were issued in Punjabi, English, and Urdu, thus ensuring that all Sikhs who could read would have access to the new ideals.

In addition to the janam-sakhi and gur-bilas styles the writers of the Singh Sabha period also inherited two differing traditions which had earlier influenced the interpretation of Sikh scripture. These were the Giani and Nirmala traditions, the former stressing strict adherence to the sacred text and the latter venturing into Vedic interpretations. The Singh Sabha writers generally favored the Giani approach, but here too the received tradition was significantly modified by intellectual ideals derived from Western sources. The combination was not always a satisfactory one, for there were features of the received tradition which proved difficult to accept in the enlightened days of the later Singh Sabha movement. It was nevertheless a reinterpretation of very substantial importance which they achieved, one marked by a notable consistency. The proof of their success is the fact that Sikh scholarship and Western perceptions of the Sikh tradition are still largely dominated by Singh Sabha interpretations.

Although the intellectual achievement of the Singh Sabha has been a truly impressive one its dominance must eventually be lost. A century is long enough for any such movement to remain unchallenged and new approaches must supplant the old if our understanding of Sikh scripture and Sikh literature is to keep pace with intellectual developments in other parts of the academic world. This will not be an easy task. Well-entrenched views are always difficult to dislodge and when the tradition happens to be associated with deeply-held religious convictions the magnitude of the task becomes truly impressive. For some people, of course, there is no real problem. If the academic need involves nothing more than description it is one which can often be discharged with little fear of indignation or offense. Literature, however, demands analysis and so too does the Sikh tradition as a whole. Challenging Singh Sabha interpretations will involve such a process and the welcome which it receives will not necessarily be a favorable one.

7

Sikhs
in the Modern World

THOSE who know India are well aware that 1947 was a traumatic year. For the Sikhs it was particularly devastating. All Punjabi communities suffered from the disorder and killing which preceded and followed independence and Partition in August 1947, but for the Sikhs the experience had a special significance. The Punjab was their homeland and the division of that homeland resulted in a total evacuation of the western portion. Muslims could take comfort from the creation of Pakistan and Hindus from the new India. Sikhs inevitably cast their lot with India, but as a result of the 1947 Partition they lost more than lives and land left in Pakistan: the birthplace of Guru Nanak and the numerous shrines associated with it were no longer accessible; the city of Lahore, Ranjit Singh's capital and the place where the fifth Guru had suffered martyrdom, had likewise become foreign territory; Panja Sahib, the famous gurdwara situated between Rawalpindi and Peshawar, was far beyond their reach. It was a disastrous year and the scars are still visible.[1]

Migration was not a new experience for the Sikhs, though previously it had been a voluntary transfer to new territories rather than a forced abandoning of the old. Many of the Sikhs who crossed to India after Partition belonged to families which had moved to the recently-developed canal colonies of Lyallpur and Montgomery districts late in the nineteenth century or early in the twentieth. Others had traveled overseas during the same period, most of them to return after several years but some to remain as the earliest representatives of the Sikh diaspora. Before examining the aftermath of Partition in the Punjab, the outlines of this movement overseas will be traced, a movement which is now producing new opportunities and new pressures within the Panth as a whole.

Sikh migration overseas is at once easy and difficult to explain.[2] It begins with the enlistment in the Indian Army during the years following the 1849 annexation of the Punjab and particularly after the uprising of 1857–58. After the latter event the British showed increasing favor towards the recruitment of Sikhs and some of those whom they recruited were subsequently posted to Singapore and Hong Kong. This revealed a range of opportunities in East and Southeast Asia, thus initiating the first stage in overseas migration. It also revealed a larger world beyond the fringe of Asia, one which included Australia and North America. Venturesome Punjabis drawn to these distant places transmitted the news and the earnings which attracted others, thus setting the well-known chain in motion.

Those who participated in this process frequently claimed that their principal reason for so doing was *garībī* or poverty.[3] In reality they were seldom, if ever, truly poor. Typically they belonged to an economic stratum of rural Punjab which could be described neither as wealthy nor as desperately poor. The wealthy had no need to seek overseas opportunities and the truly poor lacked access to the limited capital which such an enterprise demanded. Those who emigrated came from an intermediate level.

It was, however, a group with economic problems. These problems derived from such features as a falling water-table and the Jat practice of dividing a patrimony equally among all sons. Such a convention inevitably reduced some holdings to an unacceptable size and prompted the need to find supplementary resources. Social convention reinforced the need, for a diminished land-holding involved more than economic problems. It also reduced the means whereby a man could discharge essential duties (such as the marriage of daughters) in appropriate style and thus endangered his all-important *izzat* (honor or self-respect).

Military service provided one means of meeting this need and overseas employment supplied another. Those who traveled overseas for this purpose invariably planned to return to the Punjab and in practice most did so. Earnings were remitted home to the Punjab, with only a small residue retained for the simplest of living expenses. Debts could thus be paid, additional land purchased, new houses built, and daughters honorably married.

This should not suggest that mere affluence was the primary objective, nor that the individual migrant was typically feathering his own individual nest. Money can be used for various purposes and the possession of property can service differing ideals. In the case of the Sikhs who worked overseas during this early period an overriding concern was the perceived need to maintain or restore *izzat*, a term which only roughly translates as "honor" or "self-respect." *Izzat* was (and remains) a dominant ideal in Jat society and, to a lesser extent, amongst other rural castes of lesser status.[4] The possession of land is a prime criterion, together with such associated items as a brick-built house and modern implements. The scale of one's hospitality also reflects the same concern, particularly on such occasions as the marriage of a daughter. The dowry required for a daughter's marriage provides another example.

The status thus acquired was one which attached to the family rather than to the individual and decisions to emigrate overseas seem typically to have been family choices. Wives and minor children seldom joined their migrant husbands or fathers, remaining within the joint family and (in the case of the women at least) living out their lives in the Punjab. Sons commonly joined their fathers when they were old enough to do so, provided that immigration rules still permitted their entry into the same country. The pattern was one common to Hindu and Muslim Punjabis as well as to those who regarded themselves as Sikhs. In practice the Sikh group was much the largest, even when allowance is made for those whose "Sikh" identity was indistinguishable from that of their Hindu colleagues. When we talk about Punjabi emigration we are usually talking about rural Sikhs, most of them Jats. The second-largest group (well behind the Jats) consisted of outcaste Chamars.

This much of the process can be explained with relative ease. The difficult part comes when tracing the migrants to their actual homes in the Punjab. When this is done it is discovered that although the earliest travelers came from a variety of locations within the Punjab the focus soon narrows to Doaba, the plains region which lies between the Beas and Satluj rivers. Indeed the focus is even narrower. An analysis of all the Punjabis who traveled to New Zealand prior to 1921 shows that an overwhelming majority came from the three tahsils (sub-districts) which occupy the eastern corner of Doaba.[5] This small area has been the heartland for all overseas migration from the Punjab, with the principal supplements coming from the areas which are immediately adjacent to it.

Whereas the standard explanation for employment-seeking emigration can be easily applied to eastern Doaba it is much more difficult to explain why it should have applied with such force to that particular territory, leaving some other portions of the Punjab virtually unaffected. This feature is not confined to the earlier wave of emigration (the period extending from the 1870s until the 1920s). It also applies to the emigration which followed World War II.[6]

It is possible to determine precisely when overseas emigration from the Punjab began, but at least the pattern and direction are clear. As we have already noted, the earliest examples appear in East and Southeast Asia, establishing communities there which in some cases continue to the present day. Those who moved into China, the Dutch East Indies, and the Philippines left few traces, but significant groups remained in Singapore, Malaysia and Thailand. There, as later in Fiji, they are to be clearly distinguished from the indentured population or its descendants. If any Punjabis ever accepted an indenture contract the numbers must have been exceedingly small and they included no Sikhs. All Sikh arrivals entered as "free" migrants. In Southeast Asia and Hong Kong former soldiers and policemen were often able to secure employment as guards and caretakers, creating a stereotype which still survives.

While in Hong Kong and Southeast Asia Punjabis learnt of the two *ṭāpū* (islands) of Telia and Milkan. Telia was Australia and it was migration to Australia that came next. Milkan (America) was a more distant prospect and Punjabi migrants did not seek to reach it until twenty years after they had begun to enter Australia. The Australian phase, which commenced in the 1880s, provided work as hawkers and sugarcane cutters. It was a comparatively brief phase, for the colonial government of Australia soon became alarmed at growing Asian immigration and effectively legislated to block it in 1901.[7] A small Sikh community still survives, concentrated in the east-coast banana-growing town of Woolgoolga,[8] but Australia has never again permitted Asian immigration on a significant scale.

Meanwhile a few of the Australia migrants had found their way across the Tasman Sea to New Zealand. The first to make the journey arrived in or about 1890 and were followed thereafter by a small trickle. Although New Zealand was soon persuaded to follow Australia's restrictive example its earlier legislation was confined to the Chinese. It was only after World War I, when the trickle began to swell rapidly, that action was taken to block further arrivals from India.[9] This left Fiji as the only attractive destination in the South Pacific. There the door remained open until measures to close it were initiated in 1930.[10]

Well before this happened the American door had been found open and had long since shut. As far as the Punjabis were concerned Mitkan was a single place with a single range of opportunities. What this meant was that their destination was the west coast of North America where they could expect to find laboring opportunities (notably as lumbermen) in a developing new economy. The result was a movement of Punjabis into British Columbia, Washington, Oregon, and California, commencing soon after the turn of the century. Canadian and United States authorities acted independently for the most part, but their policies proved to be very similar and both governments soon began the process of blocking entry. British Columbia was actually the principal destination and it was there that dramatic events were to unfold.

It has long been believed that Punjabi interest in the possibility of migration to North America was initiated by the visit to Canada of a detachment of Sikh troops who passed through the country after parading in London for Queen Victoria's Diamond Jubilee in 1887. If interest was in fact raised by a ceremonial contingent it was probably the detachment supplied for the coronation of Edward VII in 1902.[11] The first Punjabi immigrants arrived in mid-1903 when ten men landed in British Columbia, and in the year 1903–04 a total of about thirty men entered. From forty-five arrivals in 1904–05 the number jumped to 2,124 in 1906–07 and within another year the total for the four-year period had passed 5,000.[12]

The Canadian government took action early in 1908, promulgating an Order in Council which required all immigrants to come on a "continuous journey" from their country of origin.[13] This stratagem effectively ended entry from India as no travel facilities existed for such a voyage. Attempts were made to meet or circumvent the requirements of the new policy, notably the 1914 arrival in Vancouver harbor of the ship called the *Komagata Maru*.[14] The authorities were able to frustrate most of these attempts, although the *Komagata Maru* incident involved considerable embarrassment and left an enduring memory. Wives and dependent children were admitted from 1919 onwards,[15] but in other respects Canada routinely refused Asian immigrants until after World War II.

A similar policy had meanwhile been applied in the United States. Obstacles were introduced in 1910 and a blocking procedure was regularized in 1917. The effect in each country was to leave a small remnant consisting of the few who had entered while the door was open and had chosen not to return to the Punjab. Those who remained in British Columbia could live normal family lives, though their isolation from both their homeland and the host society imposed great difficulties. For the remnant left in the United States (soon limited to California) the impact of isolation was more serious. Both communities still survive (as do those in Australia, New Zealand and Fiji), retaining an identity distinct from that of immigrants who have arrived from the Punjab since World War II.[16]

One other region to acquire a significant Sikh population prior to World War II was East Africa. Here too the first beginnings go back to an Indian Army presence, but much more important was the introduction of Indian labor to build the East African Railway. This was done between 1896 and 1901, and the labor force included many Sikhs.[17] There was, however, a notable difference distinguishing the East Africa work force from Sikh migrants to other countries. The latter, as we have noted, were predominantly Jats. For railway construction workers with artisan skills were required. Within the Panth those who belong to artisan castes together constitute the distinctively Sikh caste of Ramgarhias and it comes as no surprise to learn that a substantial majority of the Sikh settlers in East Africa were Ramgarhias.[18] This feature was later transferred to Britain following the expulsion of Indians from Uganda by Idi Amin in 1972. In the United Kingdom this group constitutes a self-contained community within the Panth, its closed identity defined both by its East African antecedents and its Ramgarhia affiliation.[19]

Britain is the last of the countries to be noted in this survey of early Sikh migration, though it should be remembered that small numbers found their way to many other places.[20] The British tale can be briefly told. Although there were Indians in the United Kingdom during the nineteenth century the first Sikhs to be clearly identified are representatives of the tiny Bhatra caste who arrived during the 1920s and worked as pedlars.[21] A few other castes were also represented, but for the United Kingdom the period of significant immigration was delayed until after World War II.

A change in British policy followed World War II because its postwar economic boom created needs which the native British were unable or unwilling to meet. The result was the flow of immigration which has transformed much of the United Kingdom. It included many Indians, and a majority of the Indian immigrants were Sikhs.[22] For rather different reasons Canada and the United States also decided to loosen the restrictions so tightly maintained during the preceding four decades. India was now an independent country and the two North American nations were both sensitive to issues involving international relations. Quota systems were eventually introduced and these have since produced new Sikh communities in both countries.

In Canada the post-war change of policy was implemented in 1951. Although the policy applied to all South Asians it was to be expected that Sikhs, with their traditions of migration and their old-established links with Canada, would figure prominently amongst the new entrants. By the mid-1980s the Sikh population in Canada was evidently 80,000–100,000, approximately thirty percent of all South Asian Canadians.[23] In Canada, as in the United States, a significant proportion of the Sikh immigrants have entered with professional qualifications or have acquired them after arrival. This distinguishes the new community from its predecessor, a contrast which is further strengthened by a greater diversity of caste backgrounds and by the preference which many have shown for eastern Canada rather than for British Columbia. Inevitably this has led to tensions in places such as Vancouver where the two waves have overlapped.

Although the weight of professional numbers makes the North American situation somewhat different from the United Kingdom all three countries now possess Sikh communities which share some common characteristics. One is the continuing importance of the gurdwara as a social center as well as a place for worship. Some Sikhs with professional skills and ambitions find their personal fulfillment elsewhere, but for most the gurdwara remains an essential component in the maintenance of valued traditions and important social linkages. In many gurd-waras the weekly langar (the meal which all take together) is a partic-ularly valuable means of sustaining such contacts within a congenial and familiar atmosphere.

Even within the gurdwaras, however, there are distinct signs that local influences are impinging and that changes are imminent. Although the gurdwara patterns of worship still replicate the traditional forms practiced in the Punjab there is evidence which indicates that the mean-ing of these forms is now being questioned by some of the second-generation Sikhs living overseas. The same questioning also extends to many of the time-honored traditions of the Panth and include an oft-repeated desire to know what the sacred scriptures actually contain.

The new communities also replicate the other standard features of panthic practice, though commonly under conditions which impose se-rious strains. Caste observance provides an obvious example. As in In-dia it is not difficult to find instances of inter-caste marriage, particu-larly amongst those from families with high-status professional or educational backgrounds. In general, however, caste continues to be observed in terms of marriage arrangements, and many gurdwaras are covertly or openly caste-based in terms of control and dominant mem-bership.[24] This is not necessarily a condition which will be accepted by the children who are now growing towards adulthood, and signs of se-rious stress have already appeared with regard to traditional marriage arrangements.

The factional character of Punjabi society also persists in the Western context, intimately associated with traditional concepts of *izzat*. West-erners who lack an understanding of these traditions may sometimes find Sikh behavior difficult to comprehend, particularly if a factional dispute happens to involve violence. Sikh elders who have been nur-tured in the tradition can be expected to cope with its results, but younger generations may well share the incomprehension of the foreigner.[25]

This treatment of the Sikh diaspora brings the discussion to the pres-ent day, bypassing the Punjab homeland and the events which have so transformed it during the four decades since Partition in 1947. I return now to 1947 in order to trace those events and to examine their effect on the Sikhs.[26]

Although the partition of the Punjab had brought incalculable suf-fering and loss it soon appeared that one notable advantage might have been acquired by the Panth. Prior to Partition the Sikhs comprised a mere twelve percent of the total Punjab population, scattered unevenly over the entire province but numerically dominant nowhere.[27] Partition altered that pattern significantly, producing the large-scale migrations which moved substantial populations across the new border. Muslims moved westwards into Pakistan, Hindus and Sikhs eastwards into India. This demographic disruption had obvious consequences for the Sikhs and in retrospect not all the results were seen to be disastrous.

Most of the Sikhs who crossed from Pakistan did not proceed far beyond the border. Although many of the refugees settled in New Delhi and some moved on to other parts of India most found their new homes in Eastern Punjab. This produced a concentration of Sikhs, further increased when the former princely states within the area merged with the Punjab in 1956.[28] Although the Sikhs were still a minority in the Punjab they obviously constituted a majority within the central and upper portion of the state. It was only the Hindu-majority districts of the southeast which made them a minority within the state as a whole.

There now existed, so it seemed, the possibility of achieving a political identity which would be distinctively Sikh. The SGPC was still intact and in 1949 the central government had conferred on it a centralized influence which it had never previously possessed. The Akali Dal had likewise survived Partition and its leaders could now survey a more promising political scene. One man stood out. This was Master Tara Singh, himself a refugee and a man deeply committed to belief in a distinctive identity. The question which confronted Tara Singh and his supporters was what political form they should seek in order to give free expression to that identity.[29]

The objective which they eventually formulated was Punjabi Suba, a redrawing of the state boundaries to include only those who claimed Punjabi as their mother tongue. In pursuing this objective Tara Singh did not lead a unified Panth. Since independence political allegiances within the Sikh community have always been divided between Congress and the Akalis, with small minorities supporting the two principal communist parties. There have, moreover, been the ever-present caste factor (one which all parties have been able to exploit) and the influence of factional alignments.[30] Jat support has been vital for all parties, and although Tara Singh was not himself a Jat he necessarily depended on the loyal assistance of Jat lieutenants. The substantial Harijan vote has also been significant. Although local pressures could often direct Harijan votes to a particular candidate the Harijan voters tended strongly to support the Congress Party as the best protector of their interests.[31]

Punjabi Suba was also opposed by powerful interests outside the Panth, notably by Jawaharlal Nehru. The claim for a redrawn Punjabi-speaking state was, in his view, a covert means of securing a Sikh-majority state and was thus to be viewed as serving the needs of the Sikh community rather than strictly linguistic. Many others shared this view, particularly those associated with the Arya Samaj and the Jan Sangh.[32] It was, however, a view which patently conflicted with the provisions of the Indian Constitution and Tara Singh could legitimately claim that opposition to Punjabi Suba should itself be treated as communal. It was a view which advocated, in effect, that the Constitution should be set aside because applying it might favor a particular community. The Constitution provided for the drawing of state boundaries on linguistic lines and if the inhabitants of a particular area were predominantly Punjabi-speaking that area could claim the right to statehood.

It is, of course, evident that the demand had a communal purpose. Those who proposed Punjabi Suba had the Constitution on their side but they also had Sikh demography in mind. They were assisted in their task by a misdirected Arya Samaj campaign to persuade Punjabi-speaking Hindus that they should declare Hindi to be their mother tongue. This set some Hindu-majority areas beyond the purview of the proposed new state, thus ensuring a Sikh majority. After Nehru's death the demand was eventually conceded, partly as a result of the conspicuous service rendered by Sikhs during the India–Pakistan War of 1965. Tara Singh had meanwhile been displaced as leader of the Punjabi Suba campaign by his principal lieutenant, Sant Fateh Singh, and it was Fateh Singh who conducted the final negotiations with Lal Bahadur Shastri. The demand was finally accepted by Shastri's successor, Indira Gandhi, in 1966.[33]

Tara Singh had provided an opportunity for his enemies when in 1961 he terminated a fast-unto-death without securing his objective, and his dismissal was accompanied by deep personal humiliation.[34] There can be little doubt that the lengthy campaign for Punjabi Suba reflected in large measure his personal strengths and weaknesses. It could justly be claimed that he was highly emotional and frequently impulsive. It must also be acknowledged that he possessed enormous powers of persistence and that he spoke a language which strongly evoked Sikh traditions and sensitivities. Although the style has always been a feature of Akali Dal strategy it would be difficult to find an exponent to equal

Master Tara Singh. No Sikh leader of recent times has matched his skills unless it be that forthright examplar of latter days, Jarnail Singh Bhindranwale.

The granting of Punjabi Suba heralded a brief period of optimism, one which has been termed "the creative half-decade."[35] An outward expression of this spirit was the series of anniversary celebrations which began in 1966–67 with the tercentenary of the birth of Guru Gobind Singh. This was followed in 1968–69 by the quincentenary of the birth of Guru Nanak and thereafter by the annual choice of some appropriate event in the Panth's history. The first two celebrations produced a particularly vibrant response, one which clearly testified to a spirit of hope and confidence. It is true that the exercise was elitist in terms of planning, conspicuous participation, and the choice of appropriate memorials. The bursts of activity produced by the various jubilees were nevertheless highly significant as a means of generating self-awareness amongst Sikhs and some important projects were initiated or extended.

Literature and education are prominent examples of the spirit which was abroad within the Panth during this brief period. In order to appreciate its influence one need only compare the number of books dealing with Sikh history and tradition which were available before and after the period began. Punjabi University in Patiala, having participated prominently in stimulating the wave of enthusiasm, benefited considerably from its result. Guru Nanak University (now Guru Nanak Dev University) was established in Amritsar by the Punjab government to mark the quincentenary occasion and it has since shown considerable imagination in the range of academic enterprises which it has initiated. An institution founded during this period with a specifically Sikh purpose is Gurmat College in Patiala. Affiliated to the Guru Gobind Singh Department of Religious Studies in Punjabi University this college prepares students for a master's degree in Sikh history, religion and philosophy. Another institution established at the same time is the Guru Nanak Foundation in New Delhi, specializing in research and Sikh musicology.

A cynical view will stress the privileged nature of these enterprises and will draw attention to the way in which they express the usual dynamics of Sikh society. Punjabi University, it is sometimes claimed, represents the Khatri-Arora interest within the Panth, ensuring that the new foundation in Amritsar would have to be a Jat university.[36] Factional alignments immediately appear within all such institutions and all are inevitably subject to a political influence which has little interest in the original ideals which they represent. Scholarship attracts little more than lip-service. Patronage, contacts and skilled maneuver are the effective means of advancement in academic institutions as anywhere else.

These are accusations which one commonly hears. Whatever truth there may be in them there can be no denying the substantial achievements which such institutions have already produced and which they continue to deliver. They have also proved to be resilient, weathering such storms as the period of Mrs. Gandhi's Emergency (1975–77) and the more recent troubles that have so conspicuously assailed the Panth.

Hints of the troubles were already becoming evident by the beginning of the 1970s. In political terms Punjabi Suba had failed to deliver the anticipated result, namely a government which would give effective expression to Sikh aspirations. In part this was because the small Sikh majority could never be mobilized for long enough to initiate any such plan; and in part it was because there was no clear consensus regarding the form which any plan should take. Punjabi Suba had provided a clear purpose, one which could be defined with precision and defended with simple arguments. But what lay beyond it? What are the special interests of the Sikhs and how should they be given statutory expression? Are these Sikhs a "nation" as many have claimed and if so what does the English word "nation" mean in this context? It may be agreed that the Punjab is the Sikh homeland, but what practical meaning should one attach to these words? During the 1980s these issues were to come into sharper focus. Throughout the preceding decade, however, there was to be much uncertainty concerning fundamental definitions and it would be idle to claim that even today the uncertainty has been eliminated within the Panth. Plainly it persists.

Uncertainties have also been prompted by the nature of the Akali Dal and by the contending elements within its declared policies. Since Independence the Akali Dal has been largely dominated by Jat landowners and inevitably it reflects their special concerns in the policies which it enunciates. The distinctive purposes of Sikh homelanders and Sikh land-owners are not always easy to separate and because both constituencies are present within the Akali Dal, grappling with the true nature and dominant concerns of the party can be a challenging task. The fact that Akali leaders have often deployed Sikh idiom and tradition to great effect merely complicates the general issue. Are we concerned with Sikh aspirations or with the economic interests of a dominant elite? Obviously we shall encounter both, but what is the nature of the mix and how does one range of objectives relate to the other?

It is a complex problem, rendered even more complex by the success of the Green Revolution in the Punjab. From one perspective the Green Revolution can be viewed as a triumph of Sikh versatility, appropriating modern techniques in order to advance a traditional occupation. From another perspective it will be seen as an alarming growth in the power of land-owners, many of whom happen to be influential members of the Akali Dal or of the factions which it produces. It also has a relevant side-effect in that one consequence has been the need for increasing supplies of labor from outside the Punjab. Many of the workers drawn from such regions as Bihar have remained in the Punjab, generating fears that their presence may alter the communal balance and increase local tensions.

The essential ambiguity of the Akali position is well expressed in a series of policy statements which the Akali Dal has issued during the past fifteen years. The first of these was the celebrated Anandpur Resolution of October 17, 1973.[37] This controversial statement begins with the claim: "The Shiromani Akali Dal is the supreme body of the Sikh Panth and as such is fully authorised to represent and lead them." It states a series of aims which include both the propagation of Sikh religion and the introduction of a just economic system, and it then supplies two lists of specific objectives. The first is confined to religious concerns. The second (headed "Political") demands that certain territories should be added to the Punjab and in item II.1(b) briefly claims a significantly enlarged state autonomy.

Economic concerns, generally absent from the Anandpur Resolution, became much more conspicuous in later statements such as the Charter of Akali Grievances issued on September 8, 1981.[38] This statement adds economic and social categories to the religious and political lists of its predecessor, and the former includes items which plainly reflect the concerns of rural land-owners. Conspicuous among these grievances (twenty-one as opposed to the fourteen claims listed as "Religious") were such items as inadequate prices for agricultural produce and a ceiling of seven hectares of rural land without any corresponding limitation on urban property. The 1981 charter is a much more strident and anxious document than the Anandpur Resolution, a change of tone produced by the political developments of the preceding decade. The 1970s were years of repeated frustration for the Akalis and these frustrations were increasingly affecting the Panth as a whole. They were certainly achievements to be recorded, notably the unique willingness of the Akali Dal to stand up to Mrs Gandhi during the period of her Emergency. A brief reward followed the ending of the Emergency, but the Akali welcome within the Janta government was at best lukewarm. When it fell they found themselves in the familiar position of disadvantaged confrontation with a Congress central government.

This brings us to the end of the decade and to political developments which were to prove dramatically significant for the Akali Dal and for the Panth as a whole. Although the events themselves and their actual purpose remain topics of vehement controversy a clear outline has emerged and some key events seem now to be generally acknowledged. One issue derives from an insistent Sikh claim that the Punjab be given a new role in Congress strategy. Together with Kashmir and Assam (both of them, like the Punjab, peripheral areas with potentially disaffected minorities) it was to serve as an example of the kind of unstable disruptive society which, if it were to remain unchecked, would threaten the very unity of India. All who treasure that unity must accordingly rally to Mrs Gandhi and her Congress government, thus ensuring electoral support sufficient to guarantee at least one more term in office.

In order to make this policy credible it was necessary (so this interpretation runs) to stir up trouble in the Punjab and to ensure that the trouble continued for as long as necessary.[39] Support for peace and stability must be publicly affirmed, but no agreement was to be reached with the Akalis. Whenever agreement seemed imminent negotiations were broken off or sabotaged in some way or other, thus increasing Akali frustrations and prompting them to actions which could only confirm the Congress analysis of the threat which they posed.

This interpretation proceeds a further step with its explanation for the induction into Punjab politics of the extremist leader Jarnail Singh Bhindranwale. Jarnail Singh was a Sant, one of the religious teachers who impart Sikh doctrine and tradition to rural Sikhs.[40] Sanjay Gandhi, having noted the increasing influence of Sants in Sikh politics, suggested that a chosen example of the breed should be introduced into the political arena in such a way that he would serve to divide Sikh forces and further frustrate the Akali leaders. This he could be depended on to do by lodging claims that would attract extremist support while embarrassing the more moderate leaders who at the time were participating in an unstable state government. Giani Zail Singh, at the time Home Minister in the central government, is also said to have been involved in the plan although he himself has vigorously denied any such connection.[41]

The actual occasion for Bhindranwale's induction was an assembly of Nirankaris held in Amritsar on April 13, 1978. The heretical Sant Nirankari sect was already the target of orthodox Sikh disapproval and such an assembly, reluctantly sanctioned by an Akali state government, was represented by Bhindranwale as altogether intolerable. The march which he led on the convention ended in a serious clash, leaving three Nirankaris and twelve Sikhs dead. Sant Jarnail Singh Bhindranwale had arrived on the political scene, and having done so he soon demonstrated that he was his own man.[42]

Bhindranwale has predictably been the object of respect and adulation, denigration and fear. A considerable hagiography has gathered around him, matched by a corresponding demonology. Although he was killed during the Indian army assault on the Golden Temple complex in June 1984 his reputation lives on, both for those who revered him and also for those who feared or despised him. An unbiased impression is, needless to say, very difficult to acquire at such close quarters and we shall have to wait until the dust settles before accurate assessments can be made. This much, however, can be affirmed. Jarnail Singh Bhindranwale has carved for himself a martyr's niche in the Panth's tradition and no amount of academic or journalistic reassessment will dislodge him from that place in the popular affections.

For many Sikhs Jarnail Singh Bhindranwale marked a return to the older traditions of piety and heroism, a visible representative of the ideal *sant-sipāhī*. In its generic sense *sant* has come to mean one who firmly upholds the religious principles of Gurmat, exemplifying in his personal life those elementary truths which the Gurus progressively taught their disciples to observe in order to achieve liberation from the cycle of transmigration. These principles include such beliefs as the eternal power of the divine Name and the absolute sanctity of the divine scripture. They also affirm the compelling power of *nām simaraṇ* and a willing acceptance of the undiminished Rahit.

Beliefs and behavior of this order characterize the *sant* and as has just been noted the word has been appropriated for teachers of popular Sikh tradition who (in theory at least) manifest such qualities. To these qualities are added the loyalty, obedience and unswerving heroism of the *sipāhī* or soldier. Although there is no sanction in Sikh doctrine for capricious or unnecessary wielding of the sword there is the clearest possible authority for its use when the Panth is assailed and when all other means of protection have failed. The authority derives from a famous couplet attributed to Guru Gobind Singh, sealed and dramatically exemplified by his own career as a military leader.[43] Upon this foundation are built the powerfully militant traditions of the eighteenth century, replete with stories of prodigious bravery, noble suffering, and willing martyrdom.

Jarnail Singh Bhindranwale has had a bad press in the West, one which effectively conceals the attraction which he exercises for many Sikhs as a genuine exemplar of the *sant-sipāhī* ideal. Some dismiss it as "fundamentalism," a word which we use when we wish to imply that reason has fled leaving a simplistic interpretation of whatever passes for basic tradition. In a sense the term is just, for Bhindranwale did indeed give expression to a strict and essentially intolerant view of the Sikh tradition. It is also legitimate to trace a part of his influence to radical uncertainties within the Panth, uncertainties which communicated the belief that a closing of orthodox ranks was vital.

"Fundamentalism" is, however, a word which may mislead, and if it is used persistently may cause to be misconstrued both the problem and the response. Like the condition which it purports to describe it can too easily suggest simplistic explanations, prompting evasion of a complex task by offering crude doctrine as a substitute. For an explanation of the problem we must take account of much more than Sikh aspirations or the militant traditions of the Khalsa. These may be relevant, but so too are the political circumstances of India's recent past and the complex range of social and economic interests which produced those circumstances.

Its strongly pejorative connotations can also encourage misunderstanding. The response has indeed involved a strong emphasis on the traditions of the Panth, but labeling it "fundamentalist" will probably ensure that our approach to the problem is unsympathetic from the outset. Bhindranwale's actions may be regarded as a gross version of the tradition, out of touch with present realities and doomed to end in disaster. His response should nevertheless be understood as a reflex which endeavored to apply traditional ideals in contemporary conditions. It should also be appreciated that those traditional ideals still retain a considerable power well beyond the circle of Bhindranwale's immediate followers.

This is not to suggest that all Sikhs will approve of Bhindranwale's style, nor that they will agree with his objectives. Violence may be endemic in rural Punjab and armed resistance may be justified when the faith is under attack, but many will acknowledge that the situation had indeed got out of hand prior to the army attack of June 1984. Although few would defend the decision to mount an assault on the Golden Temple complex it is generally accepted within the Panth that a restoration of law and order was essential. Sikhs who acknowledge this need, however, will usually maintain that primary responsibility for the crisis should be attached to the Congress Party, and they will add that a restoration of law and order must involve Congress politicians and the police as well as armed Sikhs on motor-cycles. Violence from whatever source must certainly be eliminated or at least contained.

It must also be asserted, contrary to the opinion so commonly delivered by the Western news media, that amongst those who can be regarded as Sikh leaders a substantial majority still oppose the concept of a separate and independent Khalistan.[44] This is particularly the case of the Sikhs who live in India, partly because they recognize how vulnerable the Sikhs in states other than the Punjab would be and partly because they see the proposal as unviable. Having acknowledged these differences we must nevertheless note that the events associated with the current crisis (particularly the storming of the Golden Temple complex and the events following the assassination of Mrs Gandhi) have created deep resentments within the Panth. There is a strong feeling that the Panth has been cynically exploited for purposes which do not concern the Sikhs, and that the Panth has been grievously maligned by those responsible for that exploitation or willing to be persuaded by its apologists.

Efforts which have been made since 1984 to settle the Punjab have all failed and it has become increasingly clear that real peace is probably many years and possibly several generations away. The wounds inflicted by recent years will not heal quickly, nor will suspicions, fears, and resentments suddenly dissipate. It is to be expected that these feelings will not only be encountered for quite some time to come, but will also continue to affect the attitudes and behavior of those who retain them. It has been a truly serious crisis and no one should imagine that there will be a speedy return to the situation which preceded it.

One particularly unfortunate casualty has been the relationship which subsists between Punjabi Sikhs and Punjabi Hindus. Again care must be taken not to exaggerate the damage which has occurred. One will still encounter many individual friendships which are as firm as they ever were, in some cases made stronger by the fire through which they have passed. Suspicions have nevertheless been aroused and old enmities reawakened. It is certainly to be expected that the allaying of these feelings will take a long time and that the restoration of genuine trust will take even longer.

These are negative results. On the positive side many Sikhs have rediscovered a tradition which for them was quietly fading and an identity which they had effectively renounced. There is now a much livelier awareness of the strength which the old tradition still retains and a much greater readiness to accept the exterior marks of the Panth's historic identity. Again care must be taken neither to oversimplify nor to exaggerate. It would be false to suggest that the Rahit has suddenly resumed a dominance which it had lost or that the heightened consciousness of recent years will necessarily survive a return to more peaceful circumstances. The tradition has nevertheless been revitalized and its influence on future developments within the Panth must surely have been strengthened.

For Sikhs the compensating factor has thus been awakened consciousness, a revived concern for their inherited tradition and identity. For others it is a new awareness of the Sikhs. The actual events may not have been accurately represented in all instances and for many the interest may quickly fade, but by no means all will be lost. Something of the new awareness will remain and it will be particularly welcome in countries where migrant Sikhs now form significant communities. Sikhs and the Sikh tradition have never before rated as topics of widespread interest outside India. It is a high price to pay, but if recent events can weaken indifference and diminish neglect some good will have come from the tragedy.

NOTE ON SOURCES

THERE are standard printed editions of both the Adi Granth and the Dasam Granth. All editions of the Adi Granth have a total of 1,430 pages, and all correspond exactly in terms of the material printed on individual pages. Similarly, the Dasam Granth has a total of 1,428 pages, with each page exactly the same in all printed editions. Adi Granth references give the name of a raga, sometimes preceded by the word *vār*. The number which follows the raga designates the number of the hymn, followed by the Adi Granth page on which it occurs. Where the reference is to a *vār* the first figure designates the stanza and the figure after the colon gives the number of the shalok or "couplet" which precedes that stanza. Guru Nanak's *Vār Mājh* 7:1 accordingly designates the first of the shaloks attached to the seventh stanza of the *vār* in *Mājh* raga.

In the case of the *Vārān Bhāī Gurdās* the first of the two figures indicates the *vār* and the second gives the stanza in that *vār*. For example, *Vārān Bhāī Gurdās* 26:24 refers to the twenty-fourth stanza of the twenty-sixth *vār*. When a reference to *TSSS* follows it indicates that a translation is to be found in *Textual Sources for the Study of Sikhism*.

Earlier works by the present author are frequently cited. To avoid unnecessary repetitions they will be cited by author and title at first mention and thereafter by abbreviated title only as follows:

B40 J-s	*The B40 Janam-sākhī*
CSR-n	*The Chaupā Siṅgh Rahit-nāmā*
ESC	*The Evolution of the Sikh Community*
EST	*Early Sikh Tradition*
GNSR	*Gurū Nānak and the Sikh Religion*
PNZ	*Punjabis in New Zealand*
TSSS	*Textual Sources for the Study of Sikhism*

Full publication information can be found in the Bibliography.

NOTES

2. The Origins of the Sikh Tradition

1. Wilfred Cantwell Smith, *The Meaning and End of Religion* (New York: Macmillan, 1962), pp. 66–67.

2. Harbans Singh, *Berkeley Lectures on Sikhism*, pp. 7–8.

3. M. Mujeeb, "Guru Nanak's Religion, Islam and Sikhism," in Gurmukh Nihal Singh, ed., *Guru Nanak: His Life, Times, and Teachings*, p. 116. Harbans Singh, p. 8; Professor Harbans Singh defends this view in a little more detail on p. 11.

4. W. H. McLeod, *Gurū Nānak and the Sikh Religion.*

5. The janam-sakhis are hagiographic narratives of the life of Guru Nanak, usually cast as a series of anecdotes. The existing janam-sakhis are at least a hundred years old. See chapter 6.

6. W. H. McLeod, *Early Sikh Tradition: A Study of the Janam-sakhis*, ch. 14.

7. *GNSR*, p. 146.

8. Ibid., pp. 110–12, 114–17, 125–32.

9. W. H. McLeod, "Inter-Linear Inscriptions in Sri Lanka," *South Asia* (1973), no. 3, pp. 105–6.

10. An example is J. S. Grewal, particularly in *Guru Nanak in History*.

11. M. A. Macauliffe, *The Sikh Religion*, vol. 1. The *Purātan* janam-sakhi (strictly speaking a small group of related janam-sakhis) is one of the traditional accounts of the life of Nanak, evidently recorded around the middle of the seventeenth century.

12. The *Purātan* janam-sakhi is extensively discussed in *GNSR*, pp. 36–51; McLeod, *The Evolution of the Sikh Community*, ch. 2; and *EST*, esp. pp. 22–30, 181–97. In the latter work it is labeled the *Narrative I* tradition. For the *Narrative I* tradition anecdotes included in the *B40 Janam-sākhī*, see W. H. McLeod, tr., *The B40 Janam-sākhī*, p. 11–14.

13. Vir Singh, ed., *Purātan Janam-sākhī*, 5th ed. (Amritsar: Khalsa Samachar, 1959), p. 16. *B40 J-s*, p. 21.

14. Vir Singh, ed., *Purātan Janam-sākhī*, p. 25; *GNSR*, p. 39. This feature of the janam-sakhi is set within its larger context in *EST*, p. 254–56.

15. *EST*, pp. 248–67.

16. The *B40* janam-sakhi has a poor Sikh cut his hair in order to sell it to provide hospitality to the Guru. *B40 J-s*, p. 50.

17. For a much fuller survey of the Sant tradition, see Karine Schomer and W. H. McLeod, eds., *The Sants: Studies in a Devotional Tradition of India*, esp. Charlotte Vaudeville, "*Sant Mat: Santism as the Universal Path to Sanctity*," pp. 21–40. See also *GNSR*, pp. 151–58.

18. For the Nath tradition the following works may be consulted: G. W. Briggs, *Gorakhnath and the Kanphata Yogis* (Calcutta: Oxford University Press, 1938); M. Eliade, *Yoga: Immortality and Freedom* (London: McClelland, 1958); Shashibhusan Dasgupta, *Obscure Religious Cults* (Calcutta: Firma K. L. Mukopadhyay, 1962); and the writings of Charlotte Vaudeville, esp. *Kabir*, vol. 1 (Oxford: Clarendon Press, 1974).

19. The view that Nanak's teachings utilize concepts drawn from Nath sources has been attacked by Daljeet Singh, *The Sikh Ideology*, pp. 43–66. The attack is misguided, for the author assumes that Nath concepts are said to have directly influenced Nanak in a conscious sense. The fact that Guru Nanak's works explicitly reject Nath doctrines does not mean that the followers of the Sant tradition were uninfluenced by them. The word *sahaj* provides an example; although the Sants clearly reject the Nath concept of *sahaj*, those who employ the term affirm its prime importance in its reconstituted form.

20. See chapter 6. *ESC*, pp. 60–61.

21. *GNSR*, pp. 158–61.

22. C. Shackle, "Approaches to the Persian Loans in the *Ādi Granth*," *Bulletin of the School of Oriental and African Studies* (1978), 41(1):81–96. See also J. S. Grewal, *From Guru Nanak to Maharaja Ranjit Singh*, 2d ed., pp. 6–17.

23. Guru Nanak, *Vār Mājh* 7.1. Adi Granth, pp. 140–41. Translated in W. H. McLeod, *Textual Sources for the Study of Sikhism*, p. 43.

24. Shackle, p. 93.

25. Attention is drawn to the fact that the word is italicized. It is not the English word "man." This and other key terms are discussed at greater length in chapter 4 and in *GNSR*, pp. 163–226 *pass*.

26. Linda Hess, "Three Kabir Collections: A Comparative Study," in Schomer and McLeod, eds., *The Sants*, pp. 122–23, 137.

27. In the Adi Granth all the Gurus sign their works "Nanak" and each is identified by the word *mahalā* with an appropriate number. Compositions labeled "Mahala 1" (or simply "M1") are by Guru Nanak; those labeled "Mahala 2" or "M2" are by Guru Angad, and so on. *EST*, p. 287.

3. Four Centuries of Sikh History

1. For a survey of Sikh history, see J. S. Grewal, *The Sikhs of the Punjab*. Harbans Singh's *The Heritage of the Sikhs* is written by a devout Sikh but is aware of the problems which it raises. Among the briefer surveys one which covers the history of the Guru period and the religion of the Sikhs is W. Owen Cole and Piara Singh Sambhi, *The Sikhs: Their Religious Beliefs and Practices;* it too, though cautious in its approach, is sensitive to the problems which are involved in the study of Sikh history and religion.

2. *TSSS*, pp. 9–13.

3. Surjit Singh Hans, "Historical Analysis of Sikh Literature (A.D. 1500 to 1850)" (Ph.D. dissertation, Guru Nanak Dev University, Amritsar, 1980), pp. 439–40.

4. Khushwant Singh, *A History of the Sikhs*, 1:76.

5. "Gurmat" means "the Gurus' teachings." It is inaccurately translated as "Sikhism." See chapter 4.

6. The theory has been argued in considerable detail by Richard G. Fox, *Lions of the Punjab*.

7. J. D. Cunningham, *A History of the Sikhs* (Delhi: S. Chand, 1955), p. 34.

8. The standard text is one from *Zafar-nāmā*, st. 22, Dasam Granth, p. 1390:

> chu kār az hamah hīlate dar guzaśat;
> halāl asatu buradan ba śamaśer dasat.
> (When all other means have failed,
> It is lawful to grasp the sword.)

9. Khushwant Singh, 1:88–89. For Singh Sabha examples, see Macauliffe, *The Sikh Religion*, 5:91–97. Teja Singh and Ganda Singh, *A Short History of the Sikhs*, 1:68–70. From the same period came the influential book which gave the issue its characteristic name: Gokul Chand Narang's *Transformation of Sikhism* was first published in Lahore in 1912.

10. Jagjit Singh, *Perspectives on Sikh Studies*, p. vii. The author developed his thesis in this book and in his earlier work *The Sikh Revolution*.

11. *ESC*, chs. 1 and 3.

12. Ibid., pp. 13–19, 45–52.

13. For particularly vigorous attacks on *The Evolution of the Sikh Community*, see Jagjit Singh, Daljeet Singh, and Jasbir Singh Ahluwalia in *The Journal of Sikh Studies* (February 1977), 4:36–54, 166–77; and Fauja Singh in *The Panjab Past and Present* 11.1 (April 1977) and *The Journal of Religious Studies* (Spring 1978), vol. 6. See also Jagjit Singh, *Perspectives on Sikh Studies*: the two sections of the latter title are devoted to the caste issue and Jat influence respectively.

14. *ESC*, pp. 45–50.

15. The ten Gurus were: Guru Nanak (1469–1539), Guru Angad (1504–52), Guru Amar Das (1479–1574), Guru Ram Das (1534–81), Guru Arjan (1563–1606), Guru Hargobind (1595–1644), Guru Hari Rai (1630–61), Guru Hari Krishan (1656–64), Guru Tegh Bahadur (1621–75), and Guru Gobind Singh (1666–1708). Each Guru succeeded to the title at the death of his predecessor.

16. The notable example of the egalitarian principle was the institution of the langar, the refectories attached to dharam-salas in which all devotees were expected to sit and eat without regard to caste status.

17. This evidence includes a verse by Bhai Gurdas, the distinguished Sikh responsible for the actual writing of the original Adi Granth during the time of Guru Arjan. In his celebrated *vars*, Bhai Gurdas clearly indicated unease at the change of policy initiated by the sixth Guru. *Vārān Bhāī Gurdās* 26:24. For a translation, see *TSSS*, p. 31, and chapter 6, n.33.

18. The Jats were a rural people, ranking low in the conventional caste hierarchy because they tilled the soil. This, however, does not correspond to current status, for today they are without question the dominant caste in the Punjab. They were a comparatively recent entry to the Punjab, moving up from the south and spreading eastwards into modern Uttar Pradesh. See Irfan Habib, "Jatts of Punjab and Sind," in Harbans Singh and N. Gerald Barrier, eds., *Punjab Past and Present: Essays in Honour of Dr. Ganda Singh*, pp. 72–103. In disturbances Jats were prone to violent means; they were also distinguished by their long hair.

19. This interpretation is preeminently offered by Ratan Singh Bhangu in his *Prāchīn Panth Prakāś*, sec. 16, st. 1–36, translated in *TSSS*, pp. 71–73. *Prāchīn Panth Prakāś*, which strongly stressed the divine mission of the Khalsa, was completed in 1841.

20. See for example the *Chaupā Siṅgh Rahit-nāmā*, sec. 166.
21. *TSSS*, pp. 34–37. *ESC*, pp. 14–15.
22. This is the interpretation of Sainapati in *Gur Śobhā*. J. S. Grewal, *From Guru Nanak to Maharaja Ranjit Singh*, p. 79. See chapter 5, n.6.
23. W. H. McLeod, tr., *The Chaupā Siṅgh Rahit-nāmā*.
24. Ibid., p. 150. Grewal, pp. 59–60, notes that early sources refer to "five weapons," not to "five Ks." Five is a popular number in Sikh tradition as the *pañj piāre* (the Cherished Five) and the *pañj mel* (the Spurned Five) indicate.
25. The best work dealing with the Singh Sabha movement is not yet available, but it is hoped that it will be. It is Harjot Singh Oberoi, "A World Reconstructed: Religion, Ritual, and Community Among Sikhs, 1850–1909" (Ph.D. dissertation, Australian National University, Canberra, 1987). Oberoi disputes the notion that the Panth was "decaying" during this period. For a useful summary of the period, see N. G. Barrier, *The Sikhs and Their Literature*, pp. xvii–xlv.
26. Rajiv A. Kapur, *Sikh Separatism: The Politics of Faith*, chs. 2–6. Mohinder Singh, *The Akali Movement*.

4. Sikh Doctrine

1. One work which does offer a brief theology of Gurmat is Gobind Singh Mansukhani, *Aspects of Sikhism*, chs. 2 and 3. It concentrates, however, on English terminology.
2. *B40 J-s*, pp. 45–46.
3. *GNSR*, p. 196. I am well aware that the elements I am criticizing are to be found in the earlier of my own studies. I draw attention to the years that have elapsed since then.
4. M. A. Macauliffe, *The Sikh Religion*, 3:99.
5. *Bachitar Nāṭak*, st. 2, Dasam Granth p. 39.
6. The Sants are religious teachers who communicate teachings concerning Sikh doctrine and tradition in village gurdwaras and in *ḍerās* (a Sant's abode). Young boys are sometimes sent to them for instruction and remain in a Sant's company for months or even years. The Sants are particularly strong on the traditions of the eighteenth century and commonly succeed in inculcating a firm attachment to them. W. H. McLeod, "The Meaning of *sant* in Punjabi Usage," in Karine Schomer and W. H. McLeod, eds., *The Sants*, pp. 251–63.

7. *Zafar-nāmā*, st. 22; Dasam Granth, p. 1390. See above chapter 3, n.8.

8. The term can be traced to either *gur* [*dā*] *duār* (the Guru's door) or to *gur duārā* (by means of the Guru).

5. Who Is a Sikh?

1. *Sikh Rahit Maryādā* 16th ed. (Amritsar: Shiromani Gurduara Parbandhak Kamiti, 1983), p. 8.

2. For a particularly dramatic narrative of the event, see Giani Gian Singh's account written late last century and translated in *TSSS*, p. 34–37. It should be noted that this is a traditional version of the founding of the Khalsa. See chapter 3.

3. J. S. Grewal, *From Guru Nanak to Maharaja Ranjit Singh*, pp. 86–87.

4. Ganda Singh, ed., *Hukamanāme* (Patiala: Punjabi University, 1967). Shamsher Singh Ashok, ed., *Nišān te hukamanāme* (Amritsar: Sikh Itihas Risarach Borad, 1967).

5. Randhir Singh, ed., *Prem Sumārag Granth*, 2d ed. (Jalandhar: Niu Buk Kampani, 1953), pp. 73–81.

6. *TSSS*, pp. 11–12. Grewal, *From Guru Nanak*, ch. 10. The date of *Gur Šobhā* is discussed in Ganda Singh, ed., *Šrī Gur Šobhā* (Patiala: Punjabi University, 1967), pp. 21–23. For a brief description and discussion of the gur-bilas literature see chapter 6.

7. *TSSS*, p. 74.

8. For a fuller description of these rahit-namas and a discussion of the problems which they pose, see W. H. McLeod, "The Problem of the Panjabi *rahit-nāmās*," in S. N. Mukherjee, ed., *India: History and Thought: Essays in Honour of A. L. Basham* (Calcutta: Subarnarekha, 1982), pp. 103–26. For a useful description of the important rahit-namas see Avtar Singh, *Ethics of the Sikhs*, pp. 128–45.

9. *TSSS*, p. 78. For a selection of translations from *Prašan-uttar*, the *Tanakhāh-nāmā*, and the rahit-nama of Prahilad Singh/Rai, see *TSSS*, pp. 75–79.

10. "The Problem of the Panjabi *rahit-nāmās*," p. 114.

11. Ibid., p. 112.

12. *CSR-n*.

13. Ibid., pp. 149–66, 174–90.

14. Ibid., pp. 167–74, 190–201.

15. Randhir Singh, ed., *Prem Sumārag Granth*, 2d ed. (Jalandhar: Niu Buk Kampani, 1953).

16. Gurbachan Singh Naiar, ed., *Gur ratan māl arathāt sau sākhī* (Patiala: Punjabi University, 1985), provides a critical text. Attar Singh of Bhadur, *Sakhee Book: Or the Description of Gooroo Gobind Singh's Religion and Doctrines* (Benares: 1873) is a rendering of the version current at the time of translation. See also W. H. McLeod, "The Kukas: A Millenarian Sect of the Punjab," in G. A. Wood and P. S. O'Connor, eds., *W. P. Morrell: A Tribute* (Dunedin: University of Otago Press, 1973), p. 97.

17. *CSR-n*, pp. 202–4. The portion attributed to Nand Lal begins abruptly and may perhaps be part of a longer work.

18. "The Problem of the Panjabi *rahit nāmās*," pp. 112, 117.

19. *CSR-n*, secs. 10, 543, 506, 24. A Gursikh is a Sikh of the Guru, a loyal Sikh.

20. Harjot Singh Oberoi, "A World Reconstructed: Religion, Ritual, and Community Among the Sikhs, 1850–1909" (Ph.D. dissertation, Australian National University, Canberra, 1987), pp. 176–84. The Singh Sabha was far from united on the question of Rahit reform or on the Khalsa identity in general. The Lahore Singh Sabha, led by Giani Dit Singh and Professor Gurmukh Singh, was much more active in promoting reform than the more conservative Amritsar Singh Sabha.

21. The Anand rite was developed within the Nirankari sect earlier in the nineteenth century. John C. B. Webster, *The Nirankari Sikhs* (Delhi: Macmillan, 1979), p. 16. Although the Nirankaris and Singh Sabha reformers both maintained that it replicated a pristine order, no sufficient evidence can be offered to establish this claim. The name *Anand* (or "Joy") presumably derives from the celebrated hymn of that name, part of which is recited on this occasion and others in the Panth's ritual (Guru Amar Das's *Rāmakalī Anand*, sts. 1–5 and 40, Adi Granth pp. 917–22). It does not form the centerpiece of the ceremony, however, as that place is occupied by Guru Ram Das's *Sūhī Chhant* 2, Adi Granth, pp. 773–74. For a detailed description of an earlier fire-ceremony observed by some members of the Khalsa see *Prem Sumārag Granth*, ch. 4.

22. Harjot Singh Oberoi, "From Ritual to Counter-Ritual: Rethinking the Hindu-Sikh Question, 1884–1915," in Joseph T. O'Connell et al., eds., *Sikh History and Religion in the Twentieth Century* p. 136ff. In an appendix Oberoi attaches a list of twenty-four rahit-namas or similar works, the first produced in 1884 and the last *(Guramat Prakāś Bhāg Sanskār)* in 1915.

23. Kahn Singh, *Guramat Sudhākar* (Amritsar, 1901). The most recent

edition, extensively revised, is published from the Languages Department, Punjab, in Patiala in 1970.

24. *Guramat Prakāś Bhāg Sanskār*, published by the Chief Khalsa Diwan, Amritsar, in 1915.

25. The Shiromani Gurdwara Parbandhak Committee (the SGPC) was set up in accordance with the 1925 Sikh Gurdwaras Act, with which the Akali agitation effectively ended. See chapter 3, n.26. For a study of the SGPC, see Gobinder Singh, *Religion and Politics in the Punjab*.

26. *Sikh Rahit Maryādā*, Amritsar, Shiromani Gurduara Parbandhak Kamiti, 1950, and numerous reprintings. English translations: *Rehat Maryada: A Guide to the Sikh Way of Life*, Kanwaljit Kaur and Indarjit Singh, trs. (London: Sikh Cultural Centre, 1971); *Rehat Maryada: A Guide to the Sikh Way of Life*, tr. anon. (Amritsar: Dharam Parchar Committee, SGPC, 1970). Neither of the translations is completely accurate. A translation of most of *Sikh Rahit Maryādā* is given in *TSSS*, pp. 79–86. Nine years earlier there had appeared Jogendra Singh, *Sikh Ceremonies*. This small book is, strictly speaking, a rahit-nama; as in the case of *Guramat Prakāś Bhāg Sanskār*, it incorporates routine Khalsa injunctions within its orders for initiation and marriage.

27. The only example appears to be the addition of a fifth takhat in 1963, at which time Damdama Sahib was added to the list (or acknowledged to belong to it). A takhat is a gurdwara with special authority within the Panth. See discussion in chapter 4.

28. Sainapati, *Śrī Gur Sobhā*, sec. V, st. 19.135, p. 22, and st. 30.146, p. 24. See chapter 5, n.6. *CSR-n*, secs. 54, 61, 80, 92, 145, 295, 360, etc.

29. The *Chaupā Siṅgh Rahit-nāmā* does not contain the grouping in its original text. A later text allows it, but only three of the five begin with "k" (*kachh, kirpān, kes,*). The two remaining items are *bāṇī* (the scripture) and *sādh saṅgat* (the congregation). Ibid., p. 150

30 *Śrī Gur Sobhā*, sec. V, st. 21.137, p. 22 and st. 30.146, p. 24.

31. *CSR-n*, pp. 15, 18–19.

32. Piara Singh Padam, comp., *Rahit-nāme* (Patiala: author, 1974), p. 56. Magh *vadī* 5, S.1752 = February 13, 1696. The *Prasan-uttar* of Nand Lal also gives a date in S.1752 as the time of its composition. This is not prima facie incongruous, for it does not purport to have been recorded near the time of Guru Gobind Singh's death, nor does it refer to the Khalsa. If in fact its date could be shown to be authentic the rahit-nama would assume substantial importance as a testimony to a well-developed Rahit existing prior to the inauguration of the Khalsa in S.1756 (A.D. 1699).

33. The earliest manuscript noted in Shamsher Singh Ashok, *Pañjābī hath-likhatān dī suchī*, is S.1882 (A.D. 1825).
34. According to Jodh Singh there is a reference to the Five Ks in Prahilad Singh (*Guramati niraṇay*, Ludhiana: Lahaur Buk Shap, n.d., p. 303). It is not, however, in the Piara Singh Padam version.
35. Piara Singh Padam, p. 55. *TSSS*, p. 78.
36. The two couplets reemerge in a conflated and amended form late in the nineteenth century. Gian Singh reproduced them as follows in his *Panth Prakāś* (1880):

> āgiā bhaī akāl kī tabī chalāio panth,
> sabh sikhan ko hukam hai gurū mānio garanth.
> gurū granth jī mānio pragaṭ gurān kī dehi;
> jān kā hiradā sudh hai khoj sabad main lehi.

Cited by Kapur Singh, *Parasharprasna or the Baisakhi of Guru Gobind Singh*, p. 240n. This is the form in which they are recited immediately after the conclusion of Ardas or the Sikh Prayer (ibid., pp. 449–50). Harbans Singh, *Berkeley Lectures on Sikhism*, p. 61.
37. According to the Sikh Gurdwaras Act of 1925 a Sikh is defined as follows:

"Sikh" means a person who professes the Sikh religion or, in the case of a deceased person, who professed the Sikh religion or was known to be a Sikh during his lifetime. If any question arises as to whether any living person is or is not a Sikh, he shall be deemed respectively to be or to be not a Sikh according as he makes or refuses to make in such manner as the Provincial Government may prescribe the following declaration:-
I solemnly affirm that I am a Sikh, that I believe in the Guru Granth Sahib, that I believe in the Ten Gurus, and that I have no other religion.

Most Sahaj-dharis felt excluded by the phrase "and that I have no other religion," believing themselves to be Hindu as well as Sikh.
38. Gobinder Singh, *Religion and Politics in the Punjab*, p. 80.
39. *Sikh Rahit Maryādā* (see n.1), p. 27. *TSSS*, p. 85. The testimony of the Adi Granth to *naśā* (intoxication) arouses considerable controversy. A quotation such as the following is a case in point:

> duramati madu jo pīvate bikhalīpati kamalī;
> rām rasāiṇi jo rate nānak sach amalī.

(They who consume the liquor of evil are like a Shudra's wife;
They who have drunk Ram's draught are intoxicated with truth.)
Guru Arjan, *Āsā* 114, Adi Granth, p. 399. Texts of this kind can be construed to mean either that they oppose drinking as such, or that the Gurus are comparing it to the results of the infinitely superior "Ram's draught" (the truth of Ram or Akal Purakh).

40. In Sikh sources *halāl* meat is normally referred to as *kuṭhṭhā*. *Sikh Rahit Maryādā*, p. 26. *TSSS*, p. 85. See the same sources for the ban on smoking and the offense of hair-cutting.

41. *GNSR*, pp. 224–25. The Singh Sabha did not invent the term. See *CSR-n*, secs. 53, 54, 287.

42. *ESC*, ch. 5. Examples of caste-based conventions include the custom of having only the eldest son baptized as a Khalsa Sikh, the other children to remain as Hindus. This is not a widespread custom. It is normally to be found only in families belonging to the caste group of Khatris, Aroras, and Ahluwalias, and is thus confined to only a small minority of the Panth.

6. The Literature of the Sikhs

1. Surindar Singh Kohli, *A Critical Study of Adi Granth*; *ESC*, ch. 4; *EST*, app. 7.

2. *TSSS*, p. 29–30.

3. *ESC*, pp. 60–62.

4. Ibid., pp. 74–79.

5. Ibid., pp. 70–73. *EST*, pp. 286–88. Charlotte Vaudeville, *Kabir* (Oxford: Clarendon Press, 1974), 1:58. Schomer and McLeod, eds., *The Sants*, pp. 5, 337.

6. C. Shackle, *An Introduction to the Sacred Language of the Sikhs*, p. ii.

7. C. Shackle, "The Sahaskriti Poetic Idiom in the *Ādi Granth*," *Bulletin of the School of Oriental and African Studies* (1978), 41(2):313. Professor Shackle's analysis covers a series of three *BSOAS* articles. The remaining two are " 'South-Western' Elements in the Language of the *Ādi Granth*" (1977), 40(1):36–50; and "Approaches to Persian Loans in the *Ādi Granth*" (1978), 41(1):73–96.

8. See chapter 2.

9. For Sant Bhasa or Sadhukari see *EST*, pp. 49–51. The whole of the Adi Granth is written in Gurmukhi, the script used for modern Punjabi. Gurmukhi, which is akin to Deva-nagari, was evidently developed as a traders'

script within the Khatri caste to which the Gurus all belonged. Tradition regards it as an invention of Guru Angad. This may be correct to the extent that he may have been the first Guru to apply it to the recording of devotional compositions. Because of its close association with the sacred scripture, the Gurmukhi script has acquired sacred connotations.

10. Professor Shackle defines Sahaskriti as "an amalgam of *saṃskṛta*- with *saṃskṛta*-, in other words a 'grandified speech' which recalls Sanskrit without attempting to identify itself with most of its difficulties." *BSOAS* (1978), 41(2):310.

11. This range of differing approaches is extensively described, with numerous illustrations, by Surjit Singh Hans, "Historical Analysis of Sikh Literature, A.D. 1500–1850" (Ph.D. dissertation, Guru Nanak Dev University, Amritsar, 1980), chs. 1–5, 8.

12. There is no adequate translation of the Adi Granth available in English. Of the three versions the best known is Gopal Singh, *Sri Guru-Granth Sahib*, published in four volumes. Arguably, however, the much inferior English of Manmohan Singh, *Sri Guru Granth Sahib* (8 vols., Amritsar: Shiromani Gurdwara Parbandhak Committee, 1962–69), is more useful because there is no pretense at beauty to distract the reader, and the author's system of cross-referencing individual words from the Adi Granth to the Punjabi and English translations is often helpful. The third translation, Gurbachan Singh Talib's posthumous effort (Patiala: Punjabi University, 1984–), fails in the same way as Gopal Singh. The task is, however, a forbidding one. If English is not the mother-tongue of the translator there is little hope of success, and even if it is, there is not much more. The poetry of the Adi Granth depends upon its sound as well as on its meaning, a requisite which makes the work of a translator truly daunting. The best of the translators is Khushwant Singh, notably in his *Hymns of Guru Nanak* (New Delhi: Orient Longmans, 1969) and his *Jupji: The Sikh Prayer* (London: Royal India, Pakistan, and Ceylon Society, n.d.). Khushwant Singh needs to be read with care, however, for when there is a conflict between the Gurmukhi original and the English translation, the latter sometimes wins. *Selections from the Sacred Writings of the Sikhs*, Trilochan Singh et al., trs., (London: George Allen and Unwin, 1960), is generally satisfactory, but only for readers who like a style of writing which went out of fashion several decades ago. Translations from the Adi Granth are also to be found in *TSSS*, pp. 38–55, 86–93, 96–103, 105–21.

13. For the earlier descriptions and discussions, see *ESC*, pp. 60–61 and 75–79.

14. Ibid., p. 61. Nirbhai Singh claims that photocopies exist: "The Collection of the Hymns of the *Guru Granth*" in *The Journal of Sikh Studies* (February–August 1981), 8(1–2):20, n.34. There is, however, no guarantee that these photocopies are of the original *pothīs*, which may be old but not those of 400 years ago. The work has yet to be done.

15. *ESC*, p. 62. G. L. Chopra, ed., *The Chiefs and Families of Note in the Punjab* (Lahore: Superintendent, Government Printing, Punjab, 1940), 1:167.

16. Reports were made possible while the manuscript was the subject of litigation in 1946 and access was possible through the Commissioner of Jullundur Division. The principal report to emerge from this time was Jodh Singh's *Srī Karatārpurī bīr de darśān* (Patiala: Punjabi University, 1968). Brief reports were also published by J. C. Archer, "The Bible of the Sikhs," *The Review of Religion* (January 1949), pp. 115–25; and C. H. Loehlin, *The Sikhs and Their Book* (Lucknow: Lucknow Publishing House, 1946), pp. 44–45, and "A Westerner Looks at the Kartarpur Granth," *Proceedings of the Punjab History Conference* (Patiala: Punjabi University, 1966), pp. 93–96.

17. *ESC*, pp. 77–79.

18. On the paramount importance of kirtan for Sikh worship, see G. S. Mansukhani, *Indian Classical Music and Sikh Kirtan*, esp. ch. 10.

19. *Sikh Rahit Maryādā* (see chapter 5, n.26), pp. 13–14, 18–22. *TSSS*, pp. 81–82.

20. Harbans Singh, *Berkeley Lectures on Sikhism*, pp. 58–60.

21. *Sikh Rahit Maryādā*, pp. 14–15. *TSSS*, p. 80. The term *sahaj pāth* (slow reading) is sometimes used in preference to *sādhāran paṭh*, the reason being that *sādhāran* (ordinary) is held by some to be a demeaning term.

22. John Malcolm, *Sketch of the Sikhs* (London: 1812), p. 173.

23. For further details see D. P. Ashta, *The Poetry of the Dasam Granth* (New Delhi: Arun Prakashan, 1959); C. H. Loehlin, *The Granth of Guru Gobind Singh and the Khalsa Brotherhood*, pp. 20–56; and Gobind Singh Mansukhani, *Aspects of Sikhism*, pp. 105–13. Also *TSSS*, pp. 2, 6–7, 55–63; and *ESC*, pp. 79–81.

24. Khushwant Singh, *A History of the Sikhs*, 1:316.

25. Khushwant Singh, pp. 314–17, holds this view.

26. For an exposition of a version of this radical view (with particular reference to the *Savayye*, *Bachitar Nāṭak*, and the *Zafar-nāmā*), see Surjit Singh Hans, "Historical Analysis of Sikh Literature," pp. 364–91.

27. Ibid., pp. 371–82.

28. The Nihang Sikhs, distinguished by their dark blue garments and

impressive array of steel weapons, claim to keep alive the eighteenth-century traditions of the Panth. See *TSSS*, pp. 132–33.

29. *Sikh Rahit Maryādā* illustrates the general ambivalence toward the Dasam Granth by omitting all reference to it. The term *gurbāṇī* can certainly be construed to include it and any work attributed to Guru Gobind Singh will certainly be regarded as *gurbāṇī*. It may nevertheless be significant that no reference identifies the Dasam Granth separately.

30. *Sikh Rahit Maryādā*, p. 13. *TSSS*, p. 80. For Bhai Gurdas and Bhai Nand Lal, see *TSSS*, pp. 2, 7–8, 31, 63–70.

31. Vir Singh, ed., *Kabitt Bhāī Gurdās*, 3d ed. (Amritsar: Khalsa Samachar, 1966).

32. Hazara Singh and Vir Singh, eds., *Vārān Bhāī Gurdās*, 7th ed. (Amritsar: Khalsa Samachar, 1962).

33. Ibid., 26:24. The translations for all of the passages quoted in this chapter are my own and, with the exception of note 44, are taken from *TSSS*.

34. Ibid., 36:14.

35. Ibid., 26:15. For further examples from the *vārs* of Bhai Gurdas, see *TSSS*, pp. 63–69.

36. Ganda Singh, ed., *Kulliyāt-i-Bhāī Nand Lāl Goyā* (Malakka: Sant Sohan Singh, 1963).

37. *TSSS*, p. 69.

38. For a brief survey of the janam-sakhis, see *ESC*, ch. 2. For an extended treatment see *EST*. For an English translation of a complete janam-sakhi see *B40 J-s*.

39. An example of this kind is supplied by the story concerning Baba Nanak's visit to Multan where a rose is said to have been laid on a cup of water by the earlier Sufi visitor 'Abd al-Qadir Jilani. *GNSR*, p. 142. For a discussion of the janam-sakhi debt to the Sufi model see *EST*, pp. 70–73, 82–83.

40. The various traditions are described in *EST*, ch. 3.

41. For a different approach to the life of Nanak see *GNSR*, ch. 4, esp. pp. 146–47.

42. Surjit Singh Hans, "Historical Analysis of Sikh Literature," pp. 348, 351–52, 505. Sulakhan Singh, "The Udasis Under Sikh Rule (1750–1850)" (Ph.D. dissertation, Guru Nanak Dev University, Amritsar, 1985), p. 101.

43. The exception is the *Miharbān* tradition. In the *Miharbān Janam-sākhī* each individual item is called a *gosṭ* or "discourse" rather than a *sākhī* or

"anecdote." The description is generally accurate for the bulk of the *Miharbān Janam-sākhī* comprises discourses, with considerable space devoted to scriptural quotation and lengthy commentary.

44. *B40 Janam-sākhī*, folios 188b–190a. My translation is a free one. For a more literal one see *B40 J-s*, pp. 200–1. The anecdote appears in other collections and is analyzed in *EST*, pp. 124–27. The *B40 Janam-sākhī*, recorded in A.D. 1733, draws from a variety of sources and can be regarded as the most important of the extant janam-sakhis.

45. The janam-sakhis have been extensively used in homes, in schools, and in gurdwaras for *kathā* purposes (i.e., the delivery of religious homilies).

46. Surjit S. Hans, "The *Gurbilas* in the Early Nineteenth Century," *Journal of Regional History* (1981), 2:51–53.

47. For examples, see *TSSS*, pp. 58–59, 62–63.

48. Hans, "Historical Analysis of Sikh Literature," pp. 371–72.

49. Ibid., pp. 429–30, 440–41. For a survey of the early gur-bilas literature, see Surjit Hans, "Social Transformation and the Creative Imagination in Sikhism," in Sudhir Chandra, ed., *Social Transformation and Creative Imagination* (New Delhi: Allied Publishers, 1984), pp. 99–106.

50. *TSSS* p. 12.

51. Ibid., pp. 12–13.

52. See chapter 3. For further details concerning the literary aspects of the Singh Sabha and examples of the work actually produced see *TSSS*, pp. 14–17, 133–47. Strictly speaking "Singh Sabha" should of course read "Tat Khalsa."

53. Harbans Singh, *The Heritage of the Sikhs*, pp. 226, 228, 252–54.

7. Sikhs in the Modern World

1. For an account of the disorders and migrations of 1946–47, see Khushwant Singh, *A History of the Sikhs*, vol. 2, ch. 17.

2. Particularly useful for explaining Sikh migration is T. G. Kessinger, *Vilayatpur 1848–1968*, esp. pp. 89–94. Books concentrating on the Sikhs or dealing extensively with them are A. W. Helweg, *Sikhs in England;* Marie M. de Lepervanche, *Indians in a White Australia;* Norman Buchignani and Doreen M. Indra, *Continuous Journey: A Social History of South Asians in Canada;* Parminder Bhachu, *Twice Migrants: East African Sikh Settlers in Britain;* W. H. McLeod, *Punjabis in New Zealand;* and a booklet by Gajraj Singh, *The Sikhs of Fiji* (Suva: South Pacific Social Sciences Association, n.d. but

1976 or 1977). As this list indicates the subject is attracting attention. Other titles deserving notice are two books by K. L. Gillion, *Fiji's Indian Migrants* and *The Fiji Indians;* Kernail Singh Sandhu, *Indians in Malaya* (Cambridge: Cambridge University Press, 1969); and Sinnappah Arasaratnam, *Indians in Malaysia and Singapore*, rev. ed. (Kuala Lumpur: Oxford University Press, 1979). The United States still awaits coverage of the entire area, but a recent book usefully fills an important gap. This is Bruce LaBrack, *The Sikhs of Northern California* (New York: AMS Press, 1987). See also Emily Brown, "Students, Sikhs, and Swamis: Punjabis in the United States, 1899–1914," in Harbans Singh and N. G. Barrier, eds., *Punjab Past and Present*, pp. 322–31; and Harold S. Jacoby, "Some Demographic and Social Aspects of Early East Indian Life in the United States," in Mark Juergensmeyer and N. Gerald Barrier, eds., *Sikh Studies*, pp. 159–71. A good overview of the present situation is provided by N. G. Barrier and V. A. Dusenbery, eds., *The Sikh Diaspora* (New Delhi: Manohar, forthcoming).

    3. *PNZ*, p. 23.

    4. For *izzat*, see Joyce Pettigrew, *Robber Noblemen*, pp. 58–59; and Helweg, pp. 11–33 *pass.*

    5. The three tahsils are Phillaur and Nawanshahr (Jullundur District), and Garhshankar (Hoshiarpur District).

    6. For a discussion of the problem, see *PNZ*, pp. 19–30. The eastern Doaba prominence is evidently partially related to the falling water table in the area, added to the diminished landholdings of the Doabi Jats.

    7. Kessinger, *Vilayatpur 1848–1968*, pp. 92–93.

    8. Marie de Lepervanche, *Indians in a White Australia*, pp. 12–14.

    9. *PNZ*, pp. 34–35.

    10. Gillion, *The Fiji Indians*, pp. 116–17.

    11. Buchignani and Indra, *Continuous Journey*, pp. 5–6, 14. Hugh Johnston, *The Voyage of the Komagata Maru*, p. 139.

    12. Buchignani and Indra, p. 7.

    13. Ibid., p. 23.

    14. Johnston, *The Voyage of the Komagata Maru*. The *Komagata Maru* was a Japanese vessel specially chartered to carry migrants direct from Calcutta to Vancouver, thereby getting round the new policy. However, only the passengers who could prove their Canadian domicile were permitted to come ashore. In spite of vigorous protests, the rest were prevented from landing and the ship was held under armed guard. Two months later it was forced to return across the Pacific.

    15. Buchignani and Indra, p. 66.

16. Bruce LaBrack, "Occupational Specialization Among Rural California Sikhs," *Amerasia* (1982), 9(2):45–46, 48.

17. Parminder Bhachu, *Twice Migrants*, p. 21.

18. Manjit S. Sidhu, "Sikh Immigration to Kenya" (Ahmadu Bello University, Department of Geography Seminar paper, 1983), p. 4. *ESC*, pp. 102–3; and "Ahluwalias and Ramgarhias: Two Sikh Castes," *South Asia* (October 1974), no. 4, pp. 78–90.

19. Parminder Bhachu, pp. 13–14. Bhachu's book is concerned with this community.

20. Sir Malcolm Darling, while traveling through Moga tahsil in 1931, encountered a Jat who had been in Sumatra and several who had returned from China; see his *Wisdom and Waste in the Punjab Village* (London: Oxford University Press, 1934), pp. 104–6. At least two found their way to Tonga. *PNZ*, p. 103n.

21. Roger Ballard and Catherine Ballard, "The Sikhs: The Development of South Asian Settlements in Britain," in James L. Watson, ed., *Between Two Cultures: Migrants and Minorities in Britain* (Oxford: Basil Blackwell, 1977), p. 28.

22. Rashmi Desai, *Indian Immigrants in Britain* (London: Oxford University Press, 1963), p. 19. Note that this does not include Pakistanis.

23. Buchignani and Indra, *Continuous Journey*, pp. 128–30.

24. Ibid., p. 109. Ballard and Ballard, "The Sikhs," p. 38. Parminder Bhachu, *Twice Migrants*, p. 51.

25. The same incomprehension has also been widely evident among members of the Sikh Dharma of the Western Hemisphere (the Western followers, mainly young Americans, of the Sikh teacher Harbhajan Singh Yogi). Its members typically find Punjabi values associated with *izzat* very difficult to understand or accept, just as they often disapprove of a failure to live up to strict doctrinal standards on the part of many Punjabi Sikhs. Verne A. Dusenbery, "On the Moral Sensibilities of Sikhs in North America," forthcoming in Owen Lynch and Pauline Kolenda, eds., *Consuming Passions: Emotions and Feeling in Indian Culture*. Those who belong to the Sikh Dharma of the Western Hemisphere are commonly known as "3HO" members, strictly the movement's educational branch. See John R. Hinnells, *The Penguin Dictionary of Religions* (Harmondsworth: Penguin, 1984), p. 303.

26. For a brief but very useful survey of the remaining period, see Christopher Shackle, *The Sikhs*. The account covers the entire period of Sikh history, but deals in rather more detail with the modern period.

27. Paul Wallace, "Religious and Secular Politics in the Punjab," in Paul Wallace and Surendra Chopra, eds., *Political Dynamics of Punjab*, p. 5.

28. Patiala and the other princely states of the Punjab were amalgamated to form the Patiala and East Punjab States Union (PEPSU) in 1948. Within this new state Sikhs were in a majority. It proved to be politically unstable and was accordingly brought into Punjab state in 1956. Khushwant Singh, *A History of the Sikhs*, 2:288.

29. References to Tara Singh are scattered thickly through the works dealing with the Akali movement, both before and after independence. For brief biographical notes, see Fauja Singh, *Eminent Freedom Fighters of Punjab* (Patiala: Punjabi University, 1972), pp. 231–33; and Mohinder Singh, *The Akali Movement*, p. 185.

30. Joyce Pettigrew, *Robber Noblemen*, pp. 63ff.

31. Dalip Singh, *Dynamics of Punjab Politics*, pp. 76–77.

32. The Arya Samaj was a religious and cultural body, the Jan Sangh strictly a political one. There was, however, an extensive overlap in membership. For the Jan Sangh in the Punjab, see Satya M. Rai, "The Structure of Regional Politics in the Punjab," in Paul Wallace and Surendra Chopra, eds., pp. 127–28.

33. Khushwant Singh, *A History of the Sikhs*, vol. 2, ch. 18; A. S. Narang, *Storm Over the Sutlej: The Akali Politics* (New Delhi: Gitanjali, 1983), chs. 5–6; Anup Chand Kapur, *The Punjab Crisis: An Analytical Study* (New Delhi: S. Chand, 1985), pp. 149–79.

34. Khushwant Singh, 2:299–300.

35. Harbans Singh, *Berkeley Lectures on Sikhism*, p. 62.

36. Panjab University in Chandigarh is commonly seen to be controlled by Arya Samaj interests and is called the "Mahasha University." For an illuminating (yet sympathetic) account of the working of Punjabi University, see Amrik Singh, *Asking for Trouble* (New Delhi: Vikas, 1984).

37. For a text of the Anandpur Sahib Resolution see Kuldip Nayar and Khushwant Singh, *Tragedy of Punjab*, pp. 135–37. Several versions of the Anandpur Sahib Resolution exist. This represents the 1983 version.

38. Ibid., pp. 138–39; see also the list which appears on pp. 140–41.

39. Amrik Singh, "An Approach to the Problem," and D. L. Sheth and A. S. Narang, "The Electoral Angle," in Amrik Singh, ed., *Punjab in Indian Politics*, pp. 1–28 (esp. p. 9), 129–30.

40. For the title "Sant," see chapter 4, n.6.

41. Kuldip Nayar and Khushwant Singh, p. 31. Mark Tully and Satish Jacob, *Amritsar*, pp. 57–58.

42. Ibid., pp. 58–59. On the Sant Nirankaris, see Mark Juergensmeyer, "The Radhasoami Revival of the Sant Tradition," in Schomer and McLeod, eds., *The Sants*, pp. 329–55.
43. See above, chapter 3, n.8.
44. Amrik Singh and Pritam Singh in Amrik Singh, ed., pp. 15, 178. It must be admitted, however, that this was written in 1986 and that a representative statement of Sikh opinion is quite impossible to obtain. For a view of one possible outcome, see Andrew J. Major, "Sikh Ethno-Nationalism, 1967–1984: Implications for the Congress," *South Asia* (June, December 1985), 8(1–2):176–78.

GLOSSARY

Ādi Granth	the Guru Granth Sahib, the sacred scripture of the Sikhs compiled by Guru Arjan in 1603–04.
Āhlūwālīā	a Sikh caste of the Punjab, by origin distillers but successful in acquiring a greatly elevated status.
Akāl Purakh	"the Timeless Being," God.
amrit (amṛta)	"nectar of immortality"; baptismal water used in *amrit sanskār* (q.v.).
Amrit-dhārī	a Sikh who has "taken *amrit*," i.e. an initiated member of the Khalsa (q.v.).
amrit sanskār	the initiation ceremony of the Khalsa (q.v.).
Anand rite	Sikh marriage ritual.
Arorā	a mercantile caste of the Punjab.
Bālā	one of the extant collections of janam-sakhi anecdotes, notable for the presence of Bhai Bala as Guru Nanak's regular companion.
bāṇī	works of the Gurus and other poets included in the Sikh sacred scriptures.
Bhāī	"Brother," title of respect.
bhakta	devotee; one who practices bhakti (q.v.)
bhakti	belief in, adoration of a personal god.
bīr	volume, recension.
darśan	audience; appearance before eminent person, sacred object, etc.
Dasam Granth	the scripture whose authorship is attributed to Guru Gobind Singh or his time.
dharam	the Punjabi version of dharma (q.v.).
dharam-sālā	place of worship for early Sikh Panth (later gurdwara).

dharma	panthic duty.
dig-vijaya	conquest of the world in all four directions.
Five-Ks	five items (each beginning with the initial "k") which a Sikh of the Khalsa must wear.
Granth	[the Sacred] Volume, the Adi Granth (q.v.) or Guru Granth Sahib.
granthī	custodian of a gurdwara.
gurbāṇī	works of the Gurus.
gur-bilās	"Pleasure of the Guru"; hagiographic narrative of the lives of the Gurus (esp. the sixth and the tenth) stressing their role as warriors.
gurduārā	gurdwara, Sikh temple.
Gurmat	the teachings of the Gurus.
Gursikh	a Sikh of the Guru, a loyal Sikh.
gurū	a spiritual preceptor, either a person or the divine inner voice. The ten Gurus (and their dates) are listed in the notes to chapter 3, n.15.
halāl	flesh of animal killed in accordance with the Muslim ritual whereby it is bled to death (cf. *jhaṭkā*).
haṭha-yoga	the yogic discipline practiced by adherents of the Nath (q.v.) tradition.
haumai	self-centered pride.
hukam	order.
izzat	honor, dignity, self-respect.
janam-sākhī	traditional narrative of the life of Guru Nanak.
Jaṭ	Punjabi rural caste, numerically dominant in the Panth.
jhaṭkā	flesh of an animal killed with a single blow, approved for consumption by members of the Khalsa (cf. *halāl*).
kabitt	a poetic meter.
kachh	a pair of pants, which must not extend below the knee, worn as one of the Five Ks (q.v.).
kaṅghā	wooden comb, worn as one of the Five Ks (q.v.).
Kānphaṭ yogī	"split-ear" yogi; follower of Gorakhnath, adherent of the Nath (q.v.) tradition.
karā	steel bangle, worn as one of the Five Ks (q.v.).
karāh praśād	sacramental food prepared in a large iron dish (*karāhī*).

karam (karma)	the destiny or fate of an individual, generated in accordance with the deeds performed in his/her present and past existences.
kathā	homily
kes	uncut hair, worn as one of the Five Ks (q.v.).
Kes-dhārī	a Sikh who retains the *kes* (q.v.).
Khālsā	the religious order established by Guru Gobind Singh in 1699.
khaṇḍe dī pāhul	rite of sword-baptism as initiation to the Khalsa (q.v.).
Khatrī	a mercantile caste of the Punjab (cognate form of *kṣatriya*, the warrior *varṇa*, q.v.).
kirpān	sword or dagger, worn as one of the Five Ks (q.v.).
kīrtan	singing of hymns.
laṅgar	the kitchen attached to every gurdwara from which food is served to all, regardless of caste or creed; the meal served from such a kitchen.
Mahalā	a code-word used to distinguish works by different Gurus in the Adi Granth (q.v.). Guru Nanak, as first Guru, is designated "Mahala 1" or simply "M1"; the second Guru, Angad, is designated "Mahala 2" or "M2"; etc.
man	heart/mind/soul.
mañjī	administrative subdivision of the early Panth.
masand	administrative deputy acting for the Guru.
Mazhabī	the Sikh section of the Chuhra or sweeper caste.
mīrī-pīrī	doctrine which maintains that the Guru possesses temporal (*mīrī*) as well as spiritual (*pīrī*) authority.
Monā	a Sikh who cuts his/her hair.
nām	the divine Name, a summary term expressing the total being of Akal Purakh (q.v.).
nām japaṇ	devoutly repeating the divine Name.
nām simaraṇ	the devotional practice of meditating on the divine Name or *nām* (q.v.).
Nānak-panth	the community of Nanak's followers; the early Sikh community; (later) members of the Sikh community who do not observe the discipline of the Khalsa (q.v.).

Nāth tradition	yogic tradition of considerable influence in the Punjab prior to and during the time of the early Sikh Gurus; practitioners of *haṭha-yoga* (q.v.).
Nirankār	[the One] "Without Form," a name of Akal Purakh (q.v.) used by Nanak.
nirguṇa	"without qualities," formless, not incarnated (cf. *saguṇa*).
nit-nem	the daily rule; set scriptural passages recited each day.
pañj kakke/kakkar	the Five Ks (q.v.).
pañj piāre	the "Cherished Five"; the first five Sikhs to be initiated as members of the Khalsa in 1699; five Sikhs in good standing chosen to represent a sangat (q.v.).
panth	"path" or "way," system of religious belief or practice.
Panth	The word preferred in English as well as in Punjabi usage when referring to the Sikh community (*panth* spelled with a capital "P").
Patit	an initiated Sikh who has committed one of the four gross sins (the *chār kurahit*).
pīr	the head of a Sufi (q.v.) order; a Sufi saint.
pothī	tome, volume.
Purātan	one of the extant collections of janam-sakhi anecdotes.
qaum	"a people who stand together."
Qur'ān	the Koran.
rāga	metrical mode.
rāgī	hymn-singer.
Rahit	the code of conduct of the Khalsa (q.v.).
rahit-nāmā	a recorded version of the Rahit (q.v.).
Rāmgaṛhīā	a Sikh artisan caste, predominantly drawn from the Tarkhan or carpenter caste but also including Sikhs from the blacksmith, mason and barber castes.
śabad (śabda)	Word; a hymn of the Adi Granth (q.v.).
sabhā	society, association.
sādhan	means, method [of achieving spiritual liberation].
saguṇa	"with qualities," possessing form (cf. *nirguṇa*).

sahaj	the condition of ultimate, inexpressible beatitude; the condition of ineffable bliss resulting from the practice of *nām simaraṇ* (q.v.).
Sahaj-dhārī	a non-Khalsa Sikh.
Sanātan Sikhs	conservative members of the Singh Sabha (q.v.).
saṅgat	congregation, group of devotees.
sansār	transmigration.
sant	one who knows the truth; a pious person; an adherent of the Sant (q.v.) tradition.
Sant	one renowned as a teacher of Gurmat (q.v.).
Sant Bhāṣā	the language of the Sant poets (also known as *Sādhukaṛī*).
sant-sipāhī	one who combines piety with the bravery of the soldier.
Sant tradition	a devotional tradition of north India which stressed the need for interior religion as opposed to external observance.
Sarbat Khālsā	"the entire Khalsa"; representative assembly of the Khalsa (q.v.).
sat	truth.
satinām	"The Name is Truth."
sevā	service, commonly to a gurdwara.
Singh Sabhā	reform movement initiated in 1873.
ślok	shalok; a couplet or longer composition, normally from a *vār* (q.v.) in the Adi Granth (q.v.).
Sūfī	a follower of mystical Islam.
tahsīl	sub-district
takhat	"throne"; one of the five centers of temporal authority.
Tat Khālsā	"the true Khalsa"; the radical members of the Singh Sabha (q.v.).
tīrath	place of pilgrimage with water.
Vāhigurū	"Praise to the Guru"; the modern name for God.
Vaishnava	a worshiper or devotee of Visnu.
vār	ode; a poetic form.
varṇa	the four ranks of the classical caste hierarchy.

SELECT BIBLIOGRAPHY

Ajit Singh Sarhadi. *Punjabi Suba: The Story of the Struggle*. Delhi: U. C. Kapur, 1970.

Amarjit Singh Sethi. *Universal Sikhism*. New Delhi: Hemkunt Press, 1972.

Amrik Singh, ed. *Punjab in Indian Politics: Issues and Trends*. Delhi: Ajanta Publications, 1985.

Avtar Singh. *Ethics of the Sikhs*. Patiala: Punjabi University, 1970.

Baldev Raj Nayar. *Minority Politics in the Punjab*. Princeton: Princeton University Press, 1966.

Balwant Singh Anand. *Guru Nanak: His Life Was His Message*. New Delhi: Guru Nanak Foundation, 1983.

——*Guru Nanak: Religion and Ethics*. Patiala: Punjabi University, 1968.

Banerjee, A. C. *Guru Nanak and His Times*. Patiala: Punjabi University, 1971.

——*Guru Nanak to Guru Gobind Singh*. New Delhi: Rajesh Publications, 1978.

——*The Khalsa Raj*. New Delhi: Abhinav, 1985.

Barrier, N. Gerald. *The Sikhs and Their Literature: A Guide to Tracts, Books, and Periodicals, 1849–1919*. Delhi: Manohar, 1970.

Bhagat Singh. *Sikh Polity in the Eighteenth and Nineteenth Centuries*. New Delhi: Oriental Publishers, 1978.

Brass, Paul R. *Language, Religion, and Politics in North India*. Cambridge: Cambridge University Press, 1974.

Buchignani, Norman and Doreen M. Indra. *Continuous Journey: A Social History of South Asians in Canada*. Toronto: McClelland and Stewart, 1985.

Cole, W. Owen. *The Guru in Sikhism*. London: Darton, Longman, and Todd, 1982.

——*Sikhism and Its Indian Context, 1469–1708*. London: Darton, Longman, and Todd, 1984.

Cole, W. Owen and Piara Singh Sambhi. *The Sikhs: Their Religious Beliefs and Practices*. London: Routledge and Kegan Paul, 1978.

147

Dalip Singh. *Dynamics of Punjab Politics.* New Delhi: Macmillan, 1981.

Daljeet Singh. *The Sikh Ideology.* New Delhi: Guru Nanak Foundation, 1984.

——*Sikhism: A Comparative Study of Its Theology and Mysticism.* New Delhi: Sterling, 1979.

Darshan Singh. *Indian Bhakti Tradition and Sikh Gurus.* Chandigarh: Panjab Publishers, 1968.

de Lepervanche, Marie M. *Indians in a White Australia.* Sydney: Allen and Unwin, 1984.

Dharam Pal Ashta. *The Poetry of the Dasam Granth.* New Delhi: Arun Prakashan, 1959.

Duggal, K. S. *The Sikh Gurus: Their Lives and Teachings.* New Delhi: Vikas, 1980.

Fauja Singh. *Guru Amar Das: Life and Teachings.* New Delhi: Sterling, 1979.

Fauja Singh et al. *Sikhism.* Patiala: Punjabi University, 1969.

Fox, Richard G. *Lions of the Punjab: Culture in the Making.* Berkeley and Los Angeles: University of California Press, 1985.

Ganda Singh. *A Brief Account of the Sikhs.* Amritsar: Shiromani Gurdwara Parbandhak Committee, 1966.

——*The Sikhs and Their Religion.* Redwood City: The Sikh Foundation, 1974.

Ganda Singh, ed. *Early European Accounts of the Sikhs.* Calcutta: Indian Studies Past and Present, 1962.

Gillion, K. L. *The Fiji Indians: Challenges to European Dominance, 1920–1946.* Canberra: Australian National University Press, 1977.

——*Fiji's Indian Migrants: A History to the End of Indenture in 1920.* Melbourne: Oxford University Press, 1962.

Gobind Singh Mansukhani. *Aspects of Sikhism.* New Delhi: Punjabi Writers Cooperative Industrial Society, 1982.

——*Guru Ramdas: His Life, Work, and Philosophy.* New Delhi: Oxford and IBH, 1979.

——*Indian Classical Music and Sikh Kirtan.* New Delhi: Oxford and IBH, 1982.

——*Life of Guru Nanak.* New Delhi: Guru Nanak Foundation, 1974.

Gobinder Singh. *Religion and Politics in the Punjab.* New Delhi: Deep and Deep, 1986.

Gokul Chand Narang. *Transformation of Sikhism.* 5th ed. rev. New Delhi: New Book Society of India, 1960.

Gopal Singh. *A History of the Sikh People, 1469–1978.* New Delhi: World Sikh University Press, 1979.

——*The Religion of the Sikhs.* Bombay: Asia Publishing House, 1971.

Gopal Singh, tr. *Sri Guru-Granth Sahib*. English translation of the Adi Granth, 4 vols. Delhi: Gur Das Kapur, 1962.
——tr. *Thus Spake the Tenth Master*. Patiala: Punjabi University, 1978.
Grewal, J. S. *From Guru Nanak to Maharaja Ranjit Singh*. 2d ed. rev. Amritsar: Guru Nanak Dev University Press, 1982.
——*Guru Nanak in History*. Chandigarh: Panjab University, 1969.
——*The Sikhs of the Punjab*. Cambridge: Cambridge University Press, forthcoming.
Grewal, J. S. and S. S. Bal. *Guru Gobind Singh: A Biographical Study*. Chandigarh: Panjab University, 1978.
Gurbachan Singh Talib. *Guru Nanak: His Personality and Vision*. Delhi: Gur Das Kapur, 1969.
Gurbachan Singh Talib, tr. *Sri Guru Granth Sahib*. 2 vols. continuing. English translation of the Adi Granth. Patiala: Punjabi University, 1984– .
Gurmukh Nihal Singh, ed. *Guru Nanak: His Life, Times, and Teachings*. Delhi: National Publishing House, 1969.
Hakam Singh. *Sikh Studies: A Classified Bibliography of Printed Books in English*. Patiala: Punjab Publishing House, 1982.
Harbans Singh. *Berkeley Lectures on Sikhism*. New Delhi: Guru Nanak Foundation, 1983.
——*Bhai Vir Singh*. New Delhi: Sahitya Akademi, 1972.
——*Guru Gobind Singh*. 2d ed. rev. New Delhi: Sterling, 1979.
——*Guru Nanak and the Origins of the Sikh Faith*. Bombay: Asia Publishing House, 1969.
——*Guru Tegh Bahadur*. New Delhi: Sterling, 1982.
——*The Heritage of the Sikhs*. 2d ed. rev. New Delhi: Manohar, 1983.
Harbans Singh and N. Gerald Barrier, eds. *Punjab Past and Present: Essays in Honour of Dr Ganda Singh*. Patiala: Punjabi University, 1976.
Hari Ram Gupta. *History of the Sikhs*. 3d ed. rev. 4 vols. New Delhi: Munshiram Manoharlal, 1978–84. Three more volumes forthcoming.
Helweg, A. W. *Sikhs in England: The Development of a Migrant Community*. Delhi: Oxford University Press, 1979.
Hershman, P. *Punjabi Kinship and Marriage*. Delhi: Hindustan Publishing Corporation, 1981.
Indubhusan Banerjee. *Evolution of the Khalsa*. 2 vols. Calcutta: University of Calcutta and A. Mukherjee, 1936 and 1962 respectively.
Jagjit Singh. *Perspectives on Sikh Studies*. New Delhi: Guru Nanak Foundation, 1985.
——*The Sikh Revolution*. New Delhi: Bahri, 1981.

Jeffrey, R. *What's Happening to India?* London: Macmillan, 1986.

Jodh Singh. *The Religious Philosophy of Guru Nanak: A Comparative Study with Special Reference to Siddha Gosti.* Varanasi: Motilal Banarsidass, 1983.

Jogendra Singh, comp. *Sikh Ceremonies.* Bombay: International Book House, 1941.

Johnston, Hugh. *The Voyage of the Komagata Maru: The Sikh Challenge to Canada's Colour Bar.* Delhi: Oxford University Press, 1979.

Juergensmeyer, M. and N. G. Barrier, eds. *Sikh Studies: Comparative Perspectives on a Changing Tradition.* Berkeley: Berkeley Religious Studies Series, 1979.

Kailash Chander Gulati. *The Akalis Past and Present.* New Delhi: Ashajanak, 1974.

Kapur Singh. *Parasharprasna or the Baisakhi of Guru Gobind Singh: An Exposition of Sikhism.* Jullundur: Hind Publishers, 1959.

Kessinger, Tom G. *Vilyatpur 1848–1968: Social and Economic Change in a North Indian Village.* Berkeley and Los Angeles: University of California Press, 1974.

Khushwant Singh. *A History of the Sikhs.* 2 vols. Princeton: Princeton University Press, 1963–1966.

Kuldip Nayar and Khushwant Singh. *Tragedy of Punjab: Operation Bluestar and After.* New Delhi: Vision Books, 1984.

LaBrack, Bruce. *The Sikhs of Northern California.* New York: AMS Press, 1987.

Loehlin, C. H. *The Granth of Guru Gobind Singh and the Khalsa Brotherhood.* Lucknow: Lucknow Publishing House, 1971.

——*The Sikhs and Their Scriptures.* Lucknow: Lucknow Publishing House, 1958.

Macauliffe, Max Arthur. *The Sikh Religion: Its Gurus, Sacred Writings, and Authors.* 6 vols. in 3. Oxford: Clarendon Press, 1909.

McLeod, W. H. *Early Sikh Tradition: A Study of the Janam-sakhis [EST].* Oxford: Clarendon Press, 1980.

——*The Evolution of the Sikh Community [ESC].* New Delhi: Oxford University Press, 1975; Oxford: Clarendon Press, 1976.

——*Gurū Nānak and the Sikh Religion [GNSR].* Oxford: Clarendon Press, 1968.

——*Punjabis in New Zealand. [PNZ].* Amritsar: Guru Nanak Dev University Press, 1986.

——*Who is a Sikh?* Oxford: Clarendon Press, forthcoming.

McLeod, W. H., tr. *The B40 Janam-sākhī [B40 J-s].* An English translation with introduction and annotation of India Office Library Gurmukhi manuscript *Panj.B40*, a janam-sakhi of Guru Nanak compiled in A.D. 1733. Amritsar: Guru Nanak Dev University Press. 1980.

———*The Chaupā Siṅgh Rahit-nāmā [SR-n]*. Dunedin: University of Otago Press, 1987.

McLeod, W. H., tr. and ed. *Textual Sources for the Study of Sikhism [TSSS]*. Manchester: Manchester University Press, 1984.

Madanjit Kaur. *The Golden Temple: Past and Present*. Amritsar: Guru Nanak Dev University Press, 1983.

Manmohan Singh, tr. *Sri Guru Granth Sahib*. English and Punjabi translation of the Adi Granth. 2d ed. 8 vols. Amritsar: Shiromani Gurdwara Parbandhak Committee, 1981–83.

Marenco, Ethne K. *The Transformation of Sikh Society*. Portland: HaPi Press, 1974.

Mohinder Singh. *The Akali Movement*. Delhi: Macmillan, 1978.

Niharranjan Ray. *The Sikh Gurus and the Sikh Society: A Study in Social Analysis*. Patiala: Punjabi University, 1970.

O'Connell, Joseph T. et al., eds., *Sikh History and Religion in the Twentieth Century*. Toronto: Centre for South Asian Studies, 1988.

Parminder Bhachu. *Twice Migrants: East African Sikh Settlers in Britain*. London: Tavistock, 1985.

Pettigrew, Joyce. *Robber Noblemen: A Study of the Political System of the Sikh Jats*. London: Routledge and Kegan Paul, 1975.

Rajiv A. Kapur. *Sikh Separatism: The Politics of Faith*. London: Allen and Unwin, 1986.

Ravinder G. B. Singh. *Indian Philosophical Tradition and Guru Nanak: A Study Based on the Conceptual Terminology Used in Guru Nanak's Bani*. Patiala: Punjab Publishing House, 1983.

Sahib Singh. *Guru Nanak Dev and His Teachings*. Jullundur: Raj Publishers, 1969.

Satya M. Rai. *Punjab Since Partition*. Delhi: Durga, 1986.

Schomer, Karine and W. H. McLeod, eds. *The Sants: Studies in a Devotional Tradition of India*. Berkeley: Berkeley Religious Studies Series, 1987; Delhi: Motilal Banarsidass, 1987.

Shackle, C. *An Introduction to the Sacred Language of the Sikhs*. London: School of Oriental and African Studies, 1983.

———*The Sikhs*. Rev. ed. London: Minority Rights Group, 1986.

Surindar Singh Kohli. *A Critical Study of Adi Granth*. New Delhi: Punjabi Writers' Cooperative Industrial Society, 1961.

Surinder Singh Johar. *Handbook on Sikhism*. Delhi: Vivek, 1977.

Surjit Singh Gandhi. *History of the Sikh Gurus: A Comprehensive Study*. Delhi: Gur Das Kapur, 1978.

Taran Singh, ed. *Sikh Gurus and the Indian Spiritual Thought*. Patiala: Punjabi University, 1981.

Teja Singh. *The Gurdwara Reform Movement and the Sikh Awakening*. 2d ed. Amritsar: Shiromani Gurdwara Parbandhak Committee, 1984.

——*Sikhism: Its Ideals and Institutions*. Rev. ed. Bombay: Orient Longmans, 1951.

Teja Singh and Ganda Singh. *A Short History of the Sikhs*. Bombay: Orient Longmans, 1950.

Trilochan Singh. *Guru Tegh Bahadur: Prophet and Martyr*. Delhi: Gurdwara Parbandhak Committee, 1967.

——*Life of Guru Hari Krishan*. Delhi: Delhi Sikh Gurdwara Management Committee, 1981.

Trilochan Singh et al., tr. *The Sacred Writings of the Sikhs*. London: Allen and Unwin, 1960.

Tully, Mark and Satish Jacob, *Amritsar: Mrs Gandhi's Last Battle*. London: Pan Books, 1985.

Wallace, Paul and Surendra Chopra, eds. *Political Dynamics of Punjab*. Amritsar: Guru Nanak Dev University Press, 1981.

INDEX

Man, heart/mind/spirit, 29-30
Mañjī system, 42, 143
Martial race, 8
Martyr, 38-39, 42, 102, 116
Masand (Guru's deputy), 5, 42,
 44-45, 52, 143
Mazhabi, 143
Migration, 102-10, 136-37
Miharbān Janam-sākhī, 96, 135-36
Milkan (America), 105
Mina sect, 96
Mīrī-pīrī, "temporal-spiritual
 authority," 4, 43, 51-52, 56,
 143
Mokṣa, spiritual release, 24-25
Mona Sikh, 7, 79-80, 143
Montgomery, 103
Morchā, "facing the enemy," 56
Mughals, 4, 7-8, 36, 37, 42-44,
 46, 51
Mujeeb, M., 17-18
Multan, 135
Multani, 86
Mutiny (1857-58), 103
Muslims, 8, 10, 66-67, 72-73, 86,
 102, 104, 110

Nām, divine Name, 3, 6, 30-31,
 50-51, 94, 116, 143
Namdev, 51, 85
Namdhari Sikhs, 23, 65, 129
Nām japaṇ, "repeating the Name,"
 50, 71, 143
Nām simaraṇ, "remembering the
 Name," 3, 30-31, 35, 36, 41,
 50-51, 53, 61, 63, 64, 71, 78,
 79, 87, 97, 116, 143

Nanak, Guru, 2-3, 4, 5-6, 7,
 16-31, 23, 32-33, 35, 37, 42,
 53, 60, 61, 78, 79, 102, 112;
 founder of Sikh tradition,
 16-18, 19, 22-24, 31; Hindu/
 Muslim accord, 21, 28; life
 story, 18-23, 32, 95-97, 123,
 126, 135; Muslim influence on
 works, 21, 27-29; reformer,
 38-39; relationship to Sant
 tradition, 23-31, 32, 56;
 teachings, 18-19, 22-23, 27-31,
 32, 36, 41-42, 49-51, 61, 71,
 86-87, 124; works, 19, 20-21,
 27, 31, 32, 85, 121
Nanak-panth, 4, 17, 23, 24, 41,
 51, 52, 97-98, 143
Nānak Prakāś, 74, 99
Nander, 58
Nand Lal, 64-66, 74, 82, 92,
 94-95 , 129, 135
Nand Lāl Rahit-nāmā, 65-66, 129
Narrative I tradition, 123
Naśā, "intoxication," 131-32
Nath tradition, 25-27, 124, 144
Nawanshahr tahsil, 137
Nehru, Jawaharlal, 10, 111
New Delhi, 11, 12, 110
New Zealand, 106, 107
Nihang Sikhs, 92, 134-35
Niramala tradition, 74, 100
Nirankār (name of Akal Purakh),
 29, 144
Nirankari Sikhs, 23, 127
Nirguṇa, without qualities, 23, 26,
 144
Nit-nem, daily rule, 79, 91, 144
North America, 103, 106-7, 108